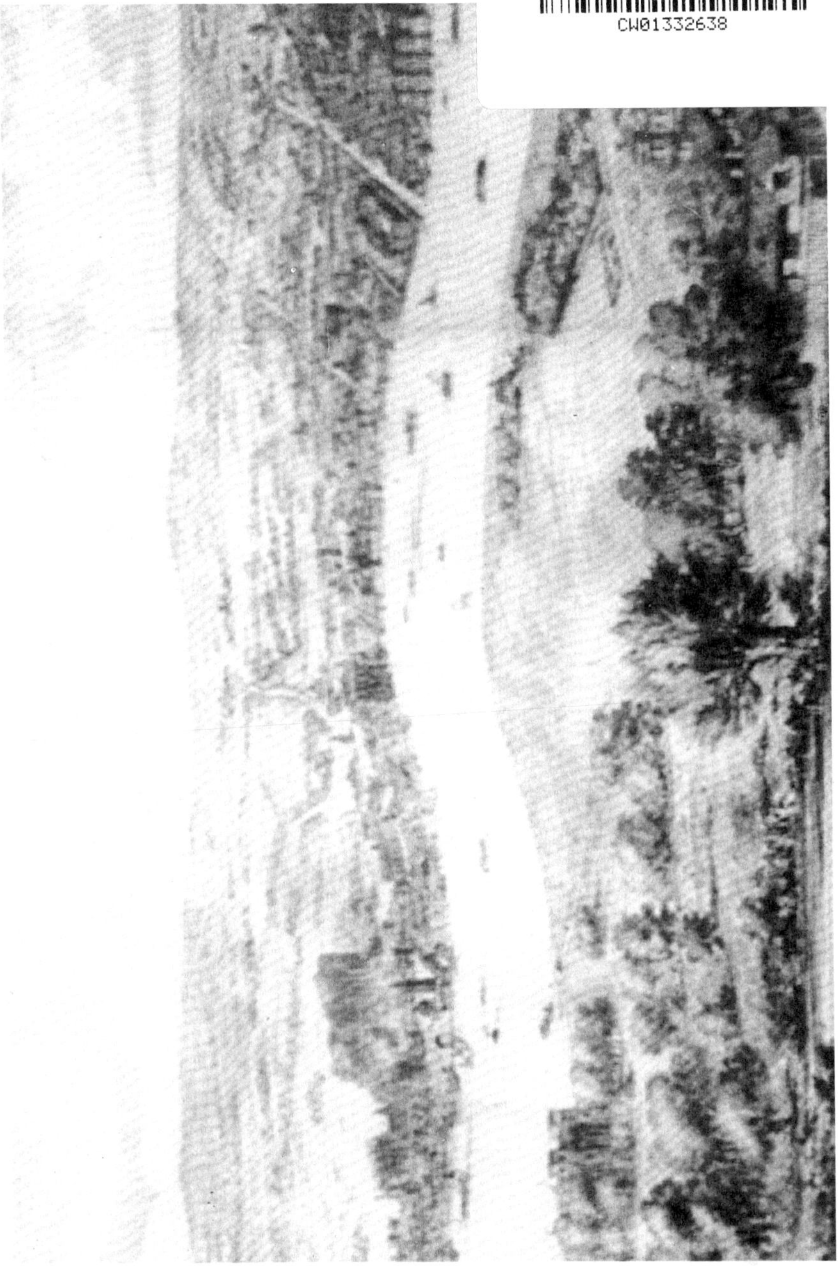

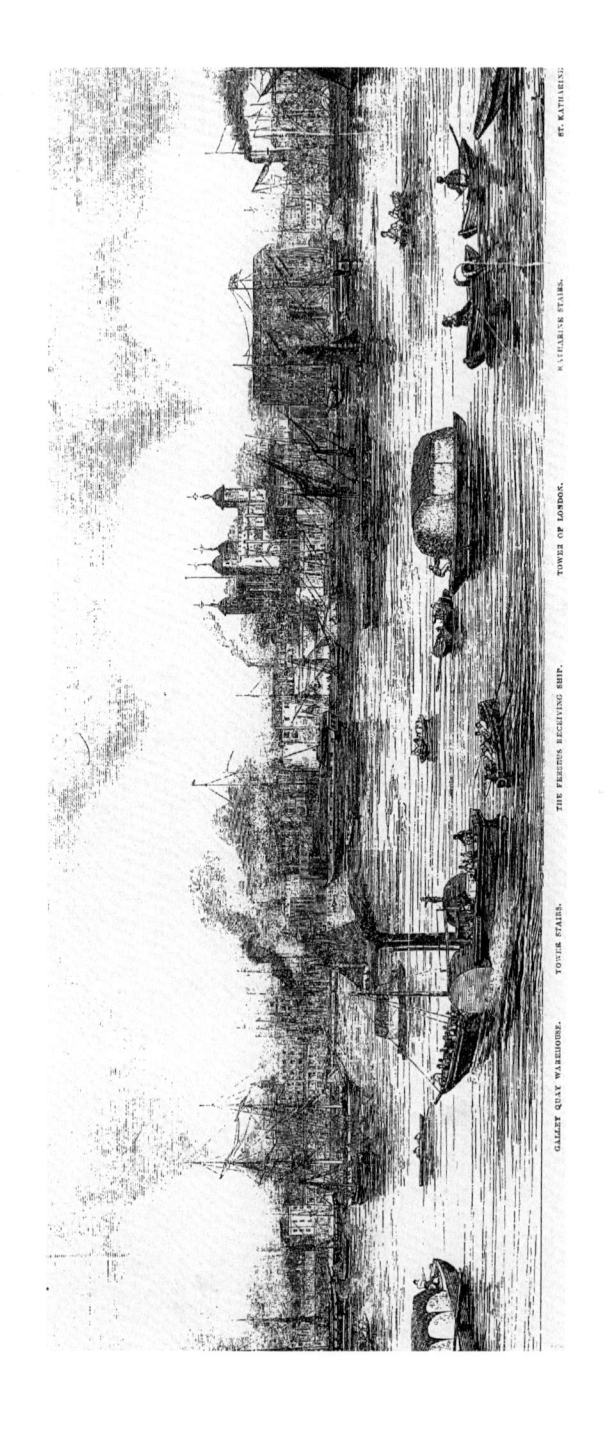

GALLEY QUAY WAREHOUSE.   TOWER STAIRS.   THE FEGASUS RECEIVING SHIP.   TOWER OF LONDON.   ST. KATHARINE'S STAIRS.

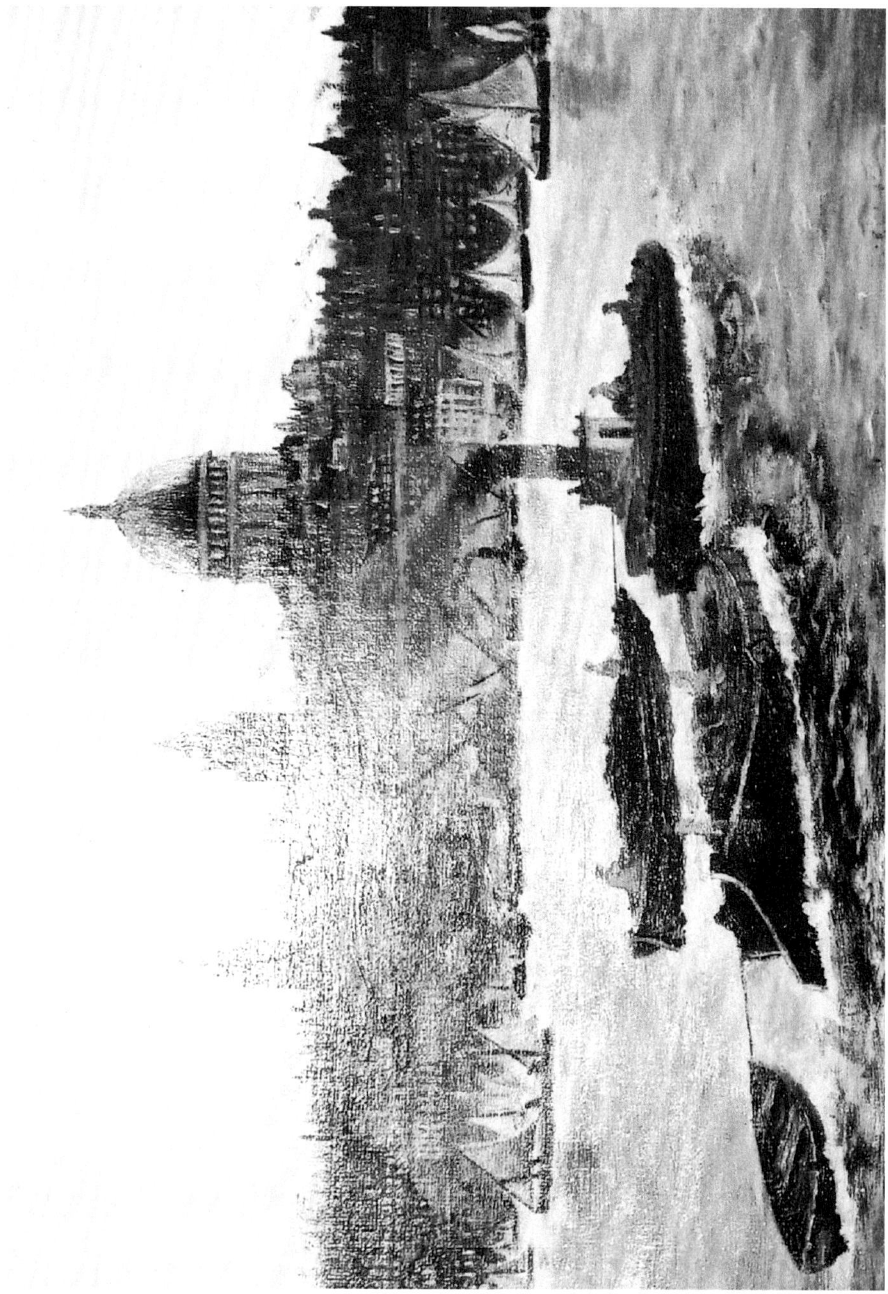

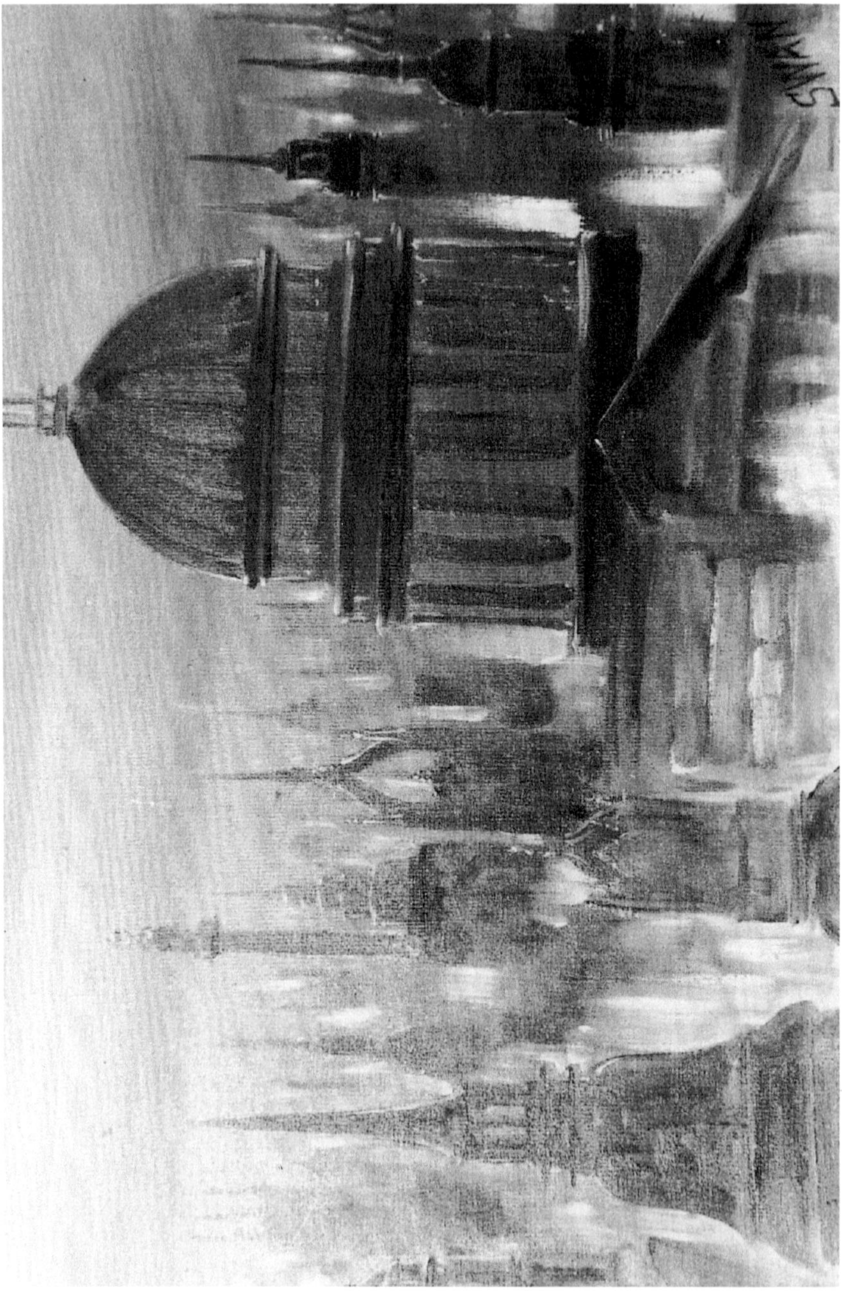

FOREWARD

How can one judge the distance of time? Many people say "Oh it only seems like yesterday" then their eyes take on a glazed look as if being transported to a different era.

Suddenly, they would jerk themselves back to the present time and with a self–conscious laugh say, "Oh! Where was I? What were we talking about?" Has this ever happened to you? Yes, of course it has.

The reason that I mention this, is, because the other day, talking to an old friend I found myself being taken back in time on a round of reminiscences "Do you remember this", and, "do you remember when"! So I thought why not bring to mind on paper all those events whether happy or sad, or even mad times; the latter word I use in a general sense and not the lunatic. These remembrances may not always be in chronological order, but there again the glory of days gone by when logged in an order as in a diary, becomes very clinical in a literary sense, and helps the theme of a dreamer of those memories.

Therefore, I ask the reader to ponder on this order of events as I recall them and not to be too critical of order but to dream along with the writer and muse to oneself "Ah! this could have been my life!" or to one not so aged, wonder whether they too would be able to revive days and nights in this way later on. This can prove to be an exciting and rewarding experience.

ST. JOSEPH'S PRIMARY SCHOOL – DOCKHEAD
(See Page 19)

MERCURY ARTICLE APRIL 11. 1996

The Mercury's pal Tom Ash recalls school gang memories during the summer and Easter holidays in SE London. Me, Georgie, Billy, Bernie, Connie and Dave - we thought we were The Dreaded Kids of cinema fame.

Basing ourselves on Billy Halop and Micky Dollanze, we spent the thirties roaming the streets singing, 'we are some of the Bermondsey boys, we are some of the boys'. It was always easier to pay for the cinema when firms had their outings. We'd go to where the charabangs were arriving back home and shout out, 'throw out your mouldies'. You could hear the pennies and halfpennies drop as they were chucked out of... the windows, hitting the road.

Summer was always the best from Easter onwards. Then those who could afford it would get a sixpenny all day on the trams and go to the fair at Greenwich. Or we'd meet at the Sugarloaf pub in Dockhead and go for a paddle down East Lane Pier, and if the tide was out we'd take off our shoes and socks and tie them round our necks. In the water we could see rubber things floating, I never knew what these were but my friends called them French letters. The older boys would go swimming near Tower Bridge. If they had no swimming costumes they'd go in the river naked, one only had one leg but he could swim like a fish. Several boys lost their lives being caught in the undercurrent in the middle of the Thames.

Often we'd meet gangs of boys from other areas and there' d be a fight. Not just fists, but sticks, stones, - anything you could lay your hands on. Then someone would call the police and you'd have to run for your life. Kids today have nothing on us in terms of home-made weapons. Catapults made in a V-shape of wood with rubber bands which fired staples. Some of the boys had slug guns which fired lead bullets. These were quite legal and could be bought in any sports shops. However, they were lethal in the wrong hands. When there were gang wars they'd be used with devastating effect. Flick knives were quite common, and most of us at least had a scout knife with many blades which we were very proud of. Often there were fights inside just one gang. To be the leader a boy had to fight for it. A boy would be selected and if he was challenged we'd gather in the square of buildings, making a circle as the pair fought with their bare fists, until one gave in and could be the leader. But a lot of other fights were caused because of your religion. I went to St Joseph's school in

Dockhead. Many a time when you hopped the wag from school you'd be walking the street when a hand would be put on your shoulder. It'd be the schoolboard man who'd be walking around the streets on the look-out for children who never went. He always wore a bowler hat and carried a brief case, and would take you back to school to be told off. But not in the Easter holidays.

Then, some who had the money would hire home-made bikes for sixpence a day from a man called Peter, who used to make them up from parts. If you did get one, you could go down to Kent for a ride. A favourite spot was Wateringbury, where you could go fishing or swimming.

Looking back I wonder how we coped riding those old wrecks and climbing up enough speed to go up Wrotham Hill on them. It was a nightmare! Swinging from one side of the road to the other trying to pick up enough speed. About half way up, sweat running down my face I would say enough is enough, and get off the bike and walk up the rest of the way. Some of the boys could get up the whole hill and you'd never hear the end of the boasting. Even going down that hill was horrible, it was so steep. To feel the bike gathering speed. They hardly had any brakes, your foot on the front wheel to try to slow it down. If there ever was a time you believed in God, then that was it praying to get down safely, seeing your young life flashing before your eyes. Then on the bottom, a huge sigh of relief.

Living by the docks us boys never go hungry. Many a time our parents had to go to the Board of Guardians near Tower Bridge when they had no food, and had to sell what possessions they had before they were given anything. But for us, there were peanuts from Chambers Wharf, oranges from Butler's and potatoes from the market.Mind you, school holidays were a nightmare for our parents.

There were many rows over children aiming stones at people's windows...while we'd be gathering in the squares to innocently play up the line with our pennies or halfpennies, tossing them up the wall. The one who used to get their coin closest to the wall won the toss. That meant placing the coins in the palm of your hands, and tossing them in the air with a clever flick of your wrist so, hopefully, most came down heads. You kept those. The ones that came down tails were tossed by the one who came second, he'd take the heads, and so on until all the coins were gone. If you could span between where they fell with your hand, then the money was yours. Another game we often played was Brag Banker, with cards, or pontoon brag. This could be quite exciting when there were quite a few halfpennies in the pot and everyone was bragging about their hands in loud voices. One boy was called Barney the Bluffer, as many a time he would win on a pair of deuces. One time when he won with a duff hand there was such a commotion all of us said we'd never play with him again. We did, though; as Barney was such a nice bloke you couldn't hold a grudge for long.

And then back to the cinema again. . . but heaven help us if it was Errol Flynn as there'd be fights galore afterwards, copying our heroes. We'd toss a coin to decide who were the heroes or villains. I hated finishing up as the Sheriff of Nottingham while someone else was Robin Hood.

When the war first started I was nearly 14 years old, my elder brother Fred got me a job at Mays Timber yard at Canal Bridge, Peckham. I was there seven weeks as a tea boy and doing odd jobs, when I collected the tea money from the men. I used to go to the coffee shop with an enamel bucket to get the tea in, sticking some of the coppers in my pocket for my picture money. I asked the lady in the coffee shop to top it up with hot water. Some time later, my brother told me that the men said it tasted like Canal water. The Foreman told me that it was time to go down the Labour Exchange to get my Unemployment Cards, only to be told when I got there that I should still be in school. Not to be deterred I told the foreman that they were putting them in the post, but after a time I came a tumble and was paid off. At this time we had what was called the false war and for a period of time there were air raid alarms going off" and nothing happening.

I lived with my mother and father in Dockhead at the time and at night we went to shelter which was in the Crypt of Dockhead Church. When the Blitz really started it was quite frightening to hear the screaming of the bombs and the noise of the Anti-Aircraft Guns. From a child I suffered from Claustrophobia and used to stand in the Crypt doorway watching the searchlights picking out the offending planes. The sky was a brilliant red with the fires in the City and the Surrey Docks. My father decided that it was far safer to go to one of the railway arches in Tooley Street, which was Stainer Street. My mother at the time decided that rather than me getting a job, I should go to queue for a place in the shelter.

I used to get a 70 Tram to London Bridge, carrying blankets to lay on and queue for a place with others. This arch was quite crowded and people laid along the kerb and in the road. Each end had large steel blast proof doors.

My father was still not happy with this so we moved on to London Bridge tube station. The Government did not want this to happen, but under pressure, they decided to allow this to happen. As soon as I came out of the shelter, I, with others, would queue at the bottom of the stairs in Joiner Street with our blankets and at four in the afternoon the doors were opened and there was a mad rush to get down to the tube station to lay our blankets along any part of the ground, where we could sleep. If you were not lucky we would sleep on the stairs or on the railway platform. Not long after this Stainer Street arches received a direct hit with a high explosive bomb, killing 60 people and wounding over 100 people. The bomb came down on 20 - 22 platform and if anyone today looks at the roof of Joiner Street, they can see were the bomb came down through the roof.

It was in the summer of 1937, my mate Georgie Saunders and myself were watching a wedding at The Holy Trinity Church in Dockhead. When the wedding went to move off we jumped on the back of the last car, sitting on the boot to get a free ride, but to our misfortune the lights were green all the way. At Tower Bridge we turned left into Tower Bridge Road passing the lights at Abbey Street with no stopping and on towards New Kent Road. At Elephant and Castle the lights were red and we were able to hop off the boot of the car, having to walk home feeling tired and scared. Never again! was one of our thoughts.

The school holidays were on! Good! Now we can go along the wharves to see if we could scrounge some oranges off the dockers at Shad Thames. It was Billy Goodwin, Terry Hill, Eddie Saunders, Georgie and myself. As we walked down to Shad Thames Billy, who really had a good throwing arm, picked up a loose stone. There were some pigeons sitting on the top ledge of the Wharf, with one mighty throw he brought one down. Looking back on this, I now see that this was cruel but as children we never saw it that way. Walking on to the steps leading to Tower Bridge we used to stand on the centre of the Bridge were the cantilevers met and as the motors went over it used to shake so much that it used to give us a thrill. Then we would watch the ships from over the side of the bridge. One time we were walking from where we had been over to the Tower of London when Billy, who was a bit of a rogue, saw a copper on the "road, shouted out 'coppers are Bastards'. With that we all ran for our lives calling Billy an idiot. On our way back we went down Mill Street in Dockhead, where, there by Reeds Wharf was a right of way leading to the Thames. It was high tide. The bigger lads, who were about 17, were going for a swim, naked. In they went. One of the lads only had one leg but could he swim, one side to the other. Another boy called Fitzsimmons, from small Copperfield House, drowned swimming near Tower Bridge.

We used to go along to the ironmongers with our pocket money to buy some twine. Going along the wharves we would pick up seed which had come out of a bag with a hole in it and with the twine we would make a running loop, putting this on the ground and some stones to hold it down. We then put the seed inside the loop, with the twine running out along the ground around the corner. The Pigeons would come down to pick up the seed, once they got inside the loop with one mighty yank we would catch a pigeon. It would fly up in the air and as it flew we would pull it in.

I was in Parkers Row one day, when Mosely and his Blackshirts were marching by. My mother came from out of nowhere grabbing my collar and saying, "come home before the trouble starts". Not knowing what she meant, I was puzzled. On the corner of Parkers Row was Oxley Street. One corner was Dean's the Grocers and on the other was the Chemist. Many a time we would go into Deans and ask if they had any broken biscuits, telling them to get some glue and stick them together. Further along Parkers Row we used to poke our heads inside the undertakers, asking if he had any empty boxes. It seems childish now but not to us at the time.

At one time, feeling hungry, I had a farthing in my pocket. I found a piece of silver paper in an empty fag packet. Putting it around the farthing, I then rubbed it on my trousers making it look like a sixpence. Walking into the fish shop, bold as brass, I asked for 'a two-penny piece of fish and a penny worth of chips please. When he had put the fish and chips in the newspaper I gave him the farthing wrapped in silver paper. When he twigged, I never moved so quick in all my life getting away.

Bermondsey Market which is situated on the corner of Long Lane | and Tower Bridge Road, was transferred there from the old Caledonian Market in

Caledonian Road, and on a Friday you cart see dealers and members of the public mingling among the stalls. Even if you have no money to spend it is quite a pleasure to see pieces of Dresden and Meissen Derby and; Staffordshire figures in Antiques. You name it, they have it*-Silver, paintings, old lamps, old pieces of furniture, clocks and watches, beautiful Georgian glass, jewellery and even old books.

A lot of the stall holders go there in the their motors on Thursday nights. Even though it is against the law, you could see quite a few of them dealing off the back of their vans, selling to the shippers from all parts of the world. Most of the stallholders came from all over the country. A lot were from Brighton and quite a few from Kent. These used to come up in their vans or cars and sleep in their vehicles overnight because it was more convenient than travelling early in the morning. Many a time you could see the boys who do on the knocker buying from door to door arriving with their lorries loaded with old furniture and all the dealers would rush to see what they could buy. The Police were very busy trying to catch these wide boys, but as soon as they saw the Police they shut the back of the van and could not be touched unless they were actually caught in the act of taking money.

Whilst working in the Swedish yard, when I was a Docker, I was hit on the head by a crane hook and landed up in Guys Hospital. I was there as an outpatient for several years. As I was not getting any better the Doctor said to me 'have you any hobbies? 'No' I replied. 'Well you had better get yourself a hobby' he said.

A Stevedore that I knew in the Surreys was always speaking about the books he had on Bermondsey. So I thought to myself, I will try to emulate him with books on local history. But where can I get these books? So I tried down the Bermondsey Market, as I knew most of the stallholders. One Friday when walking round, I went into the white buildings on the corner of Bermondsey Street. In here there were stalls and rooms full of antiques and as I was talking to a dealer about what I was looking for he said to me 'I have a little book on London' 'Good John, can I have a look?' I asked. It was a very old book - Richard Burton's new view on London 1732. It was only a small book with curious wood engravings.

'I'm not sure I want to sell it' said John 'come on John' I said 'Its no good to you, your not a book man1 and so he let me have it for five pounds, which gave me great excitement. After this I found myself going around various bookshops whenever I got a 'bomper'. The next Step was a small bookshop in Tranquil Vale, Blackheath, where I purchased a copy of Clarke's History of Bermondsey which was published in 1909, I was very pleased with this purchase. I next went to a place were I bought Walford's Old and New London for thirty shillings, which is in six volumes. These are very good books and are very underrated. They are full of very good wood engravings. I don't know why but wood engravings are not much sought after. I soon found that this Stevedore Waffy as he was called, considered me a rival and he said to me one day 'you can't find a copy of Beck's History of Rotherhithe?' and said that he possessed a copy. I thought to myself whatever book he buys he will always say to me that I cannot get that book. So I set myself the task of getting this book. Up and down the bookstalls in Farringdon Street, in all the little bookshops in Charing Cross Road. The same answer 'no I'm sorry'. I soon found although this book is like finding a gold brick in the road, it was not a rare book but was scarce not worth a lot of money at the time. Just when I was about to give up, I remembered Stanley Crows of Bloomsbury.

'I'll call in there I said to myself. It was a curious shop at the back of the British Museum. I climbed the steps and walked inside. I said 'good morning' to the woman in charge. She said 'I have something for you' and with this she pulled out a book from under the counter - Beck's History of Rotherhithe - she knew I was searching for this book and had put it aside for me.

I could have jumped for joy. It cost me 7 pounds, at last no more taunting about this book, I had a copy! Strange thing was that now the hunt was over, I realised that the thrill was more in searching for this book for so long. I found three more copies of this book. I bought these books as I found that scarce books are very good for bartering. The next set of books I bought were Knighted London.

They say the hardest thing in life is making a choice. I found out to my cost, one Friday, when I went to Bermondsey Market. A woman I know offered me Maitland's survey of London 1760 for 20 pounds. As I was bomping on and was not certain of the Wife's money I balked and regretted it to this day as it is now worth well over 100 pounds. Another book I was lucky to buy was Nathaniel Dews History of Deptford 1883. This one came from the Evlyn family and was also signed by one of the family.

CHAPTER 1

When I was young in the 30's we used to make our own amusements because our parents had no money to spare. On Sunday mornings we would play up the line with our pennies, tossing them up against the building wall. The one who got the closest then tossed the coins up in the air and waited till all the coins settled and then looked to see how many of them were heads and how many were tails. The one who tossed was heads and took all that came down heads and the other person would take those that came down tails. Another game with coins was 'spansy'. This was similar to the previous game in that you tossed the coins up to the wall of the building then the other person would have to toss his coins and then try to span with his hand to the other persons coins. If he could do this then he won the money. Card schools were held in the drying rooms of the buildings situated at the top of our buildings. Brag was my favourite game also banker. The girls would be playing hop scotch in the square and skipping was a favourite pastime with them. Tops and whips were pretty evident at this time. Can't see many children playing with these sort of toys now as the traffic won't allow them. We could 'spike our tops in the kerb and with a home-made whip (usually a shoe lace tied on to a stick of wood) wind it round the top and spin off then would come the testing period of seeing how many times one would have to whip the top to keep it spinning. I could go on for ever over the games we played. Another loved sport was marbles. We each had our lucky marble. One we would hardly ever use except in an emergency when we would be losing then out would come our 'lucky' and wham! then watch it mate, off we go in the gutter along the kerb pinking the glass balls and picking off the other kids best glass eyes. The bigger marbles were sixers as you would have to hit it six times before you could win it. Many's the time we would go along to Cherry Garden Pier climb onto the barges to see what was on them. At Chambers you could always rely on some peanuts. The water in the river was nice and clean then and you could see the sticklebacks swimming in the water and on the really nice warm days in the summer we would go swimming in the Thames. People would sit up on the side of the river at Platform wharf and watch us. They would take sandwiches and make a picnic of it. My old man had a cricket bat and we used to go and play in the 'cage' as it was known. This was a square in the middle of the buildings and was surrounded by high wire fencing so that our balls would not smash any of the windows. There was a copper called Irish Mike and he would sneak up on us if he caught anyone he would not nick them but would take off his belt and wallop their bottoms playfully. Poor 'ole Mike, he was not quick on his pins and had a job to catch us. Another game that comes to mind was leapfrogging. There were these posts that lined the side of the road and we would happily leap-frog over them. Many is the time that I misjudged the height blimey did I shout.

  I was always envious of Billy Goodwin who could throw a tennis ball over the top of the buildings from one side to the other. I could only manage to throw as high as the top windows. Many a time a window would go up and someone holler out and shouting "Wait till I see your mother you won't 'alf cop it". Billy was also good at catching birds (feather variety) we would climb over the fence to the bomb site next to the fire station at Dockhead and with 3 old bricks 3 pieces of wood and a bit of stale bread. Breaking one brick in half placing one brick either side and half a brick one side and half the other making a box, one piece of wood in the ground another piece across it and the other piece standing on top to support the last remaining brick across the top when the bird came down to take the bread on the stick this dislodged the stick holding up the top brick bringing down the brick and trapping the bird.

  On Guy Fawkes night we were lucky for Terry Hills who was one of my mates used to get quite a lot of fireworks. The delight in seeing the skyrockets and 'war in the Air' they would go soaring up into the air and explode about six times woom, woom, woom on it would go.

I remember one day when we were happily playing and the R101 Airship went over our heads. It was so low that you could see the Gondola underneath and the big R101 on the nose. To us youngsters it was very exciting.

Then there was the time that the Crystal Palace caught fire. What a luvverly blaze that was and what excitement. I remember it well. We were at the 'Time and Talents' club in George Row on the corner of Marine Street and Abbey Street, when someone shouted "The Crystal Palace is on fire". We all raced to the buildings and got to the top of them and we all had a glorious view of the fire. This I shall never forget.

"One two three a lairy, my balls down the airy," this was a chant that one could hear in every street where the kids would be playing with brightly coloured balls. Some big, and some small, legs swinging over the bounce of the ball, first the right then the left. If you caught the ball with your leg then you were 'out'. A piece of old rope (probably mums washing line used for the occasion) was a girls delight. All the chants as each girl would take turns in skipping. Competition was rife to see who could skip the longest without 'getting out'. If the boys skipped they would be called a sissy by the other boys.

Bikes was another useful asset as we would race one another on these old made up two wheelers. I will always remember Peter who had a place down an airey in East Lane who used to hire out old bikes for 6 pence a day. They were old bikes, I should say they were! no brakes on them one would have to use your foot on the front wheel to brake this was easy as they had no mudguards on them either. But no matter we enjoyed this daring piece of old iron. Scooters was another of Peter's assets. These were made up from two planks of wood with a block on one of them to hold the eye screws the other would have two more eye screws and you would lay these one on top of the other and then a long bolt would go through them and tightened up with a nut. At the base of the upright plank a triangle was cut out where the ball-bearing wheel would be inserted. On the other end of the horizontal plank another triangle was cut out to hold the other wheel. When this was assembled, one would have a lovely piece of transport.

On Saturdays we would go round to Lloyds the tin box makers in the winter which was in Mill Street and going into the yard picking up all the old wood and chopping it up into sticks and making them into bundles we would then hawk the firewood around the doors at ha'penny a time. This would get our picture money. Ah! what joy this conjures up. There were many 'picture' houses in Bermondsey. There was the Star, affectionately known as the Rats in Backslang this was in Abbey Street, Trocette, Old Kent, Globe and the Stork. The Grange was naturally in Grange Road. These were our favourite haunts and who could ever forget the Hippodrome or the Hip as it was known. Many's the time we have 'bunked into the Gods' for the cheapest seats were near the roof and one would be seated on stone seats, most uncomfortable but this was soon forgotten as our favourite heroes would come bounding onto the screen. Tom Mix, Buck Jones, Gene Autry and the never to be forgotten Flash Gordon. These would take us out of our drab existence and transport us into our fantasy world where we would all be the heroes. When Erroll Flynn came on the screen in The Charge of the Light Brigade and the music blared out the stomping of hundreds of kids feet was quite deafening. If you were unlucky enough to get a seat that was behind the supporting pillars you would get a crick in the neck trying to see around it, and one would hear a roar from behind "Oi get yer big 'ead out of it".

Our nearest park playground was Southwark Park. This was some distance away from where we lived but we would often go there to the open air swimming baths in the summer. It was closed in the winter. On the greens the old men would be playing bowls and we would watch them. Then there were the swings and rounders. These were big posts which had ropes coming down the sides joined to a moving part and as you gave a little run and then jumped up into the air supporting your arm in the sling part of the rope you could go round and round on this particular appliance for a long time. Many boys would watch the girls on these rounders as they would go up in the air and we would strain our eyes to try and see what coloured knickers they had on. This was harder than you would expect as the girls would invariably tuck the end of their dresses or skirts into the legs of their knickers. Now and again you would get a daring miss who delighted in tormenting us boys with glimpses of leg and edge of navy blue.

You know, Bermondsey is not a bad place as is made out. There have been quite a few men who have 'done us proud'. There was the man from Keeton's Road who won the V.C. and another the Military Cross. Tommy Steele is the one in the present who 'made it good' and from the other end, although not quite Bermondsey is Max Bygraves.

Bermondsey has quite a lot of history attached to it, there was in the first instance the famous Bermondsey Abbey, Abbey Street is so named as being the site of this famous of buildings. This was where the first Queen Elizabeth was imprisoned before she became queen.

"The old place ain't wot it used ter be" motor traffic was rare as the streets would be chock a block with horse drawn carts together with the trams on the tram lines in the middle of the road. These were very hazardous as there were a lot of winding turnings along the length of road leading from London Bridge to Greenwich Church and the other route from Waterloo to Greenwich. But what fun to ride on these vehicles as they careered along. One would hold ones 'heart in their mouths'. Another thing was the horse and carts. A favourite pastime would be for us to jump onto the tailboard of these passing vehicles and stay there until someone would shout to the driver "look be'ind you guvnor" then the driver would shout at us "gerroff you buggers" and a loud crack would issue from his whip at which we would nip smartly off the cart.

I had a friend called Barney who had a reputation of being the greatest 'gobber'. He could 'throw a gob' at least 12 feet. I remember on one occasion when we had one of our 'card schools' and we were playing brag, Barney landed an almighty 'gob' on the ceiling and there it hung very menacingly over the cards. There was one hell of a rush to pick up the cards and money before the gob landed. "You dirty b......" and amid the laughter we all ran down the stairs.

We had our heroes in those days. One of these great men was Ron Johnson, who used to ride for the New Cross Speedway. This was our local track and when we could make it we would go there just to watch these exciting men go round and round on the track. Holding our breath, waiting for the spills that go with this dangerous and exhillerating sport. Then there was Don Bradman, who was one of the few private heroes of mine. Usually, down our way, anyone who was interested in the sports field would either go along to their local track or field and generally speaking, support the local team to the death. Lo and behold anyone who was against the 'locals'. If a mate got a bit stroppy we would all cry out "who do you think you are, Jack Johnson"! Another of these 'giants' was Sir Malcolm Campbell. To us lads when he broke the land speed record we broke into great cheers. We would avidly collect the cigarette cards of all our favourites. Many's the time my mates would craftily buy between them a packet of fags for the cards inside them and often when seeing a grown-up walking along smoking, would ask smilingly "got any cards mister". Usually one would stop and take out his packet and say "here you are sonny". If we got any 'doubles' we would gather together and do a swap, this gave us a particularly good pastime and our mothers were pleased to see us keep out of 'trouble'.

Remembering as I am writing pictures keep flashing through my mind and it is difficult to sort out like a movie that has the reels the wrong way round. I suddenly see a picture of the stables of Potter Priestly's. This was a haulage company that had many horse-drawn carts which we would jump on and off as they went past. Two great big horses, sometimes they would slip and slide on the cobbled streets giving off sparks as their hooves clattered to steady themselves, tugging away with what seemed to us loads on the carts too much even for these creatures to handle. Crack! The drivers whip would lash out across the horses backs if they were a bit slow in pulling the cart away. At this we would shout and jump up at the cart trying to get at the driver and try and take the whip away. Had we looked a little closer we would have seen that the lash did not strike the horse but merely let out a loud noise. Sometimes there was some cruel men but we never seemed to see them around much as there was bound to be somebody who would report whether these dumb animals were being ill-treated.

Potter Priestly's Cartage co. had their place in Marine Street, just off George Row, and here on the corner there was a drinking trough where the horses would get a drink either before starting on their journeys or when returning, especially if they were waiting to get into the yard. In this trough you could see goldfish. Yes, goldfish! Many a time my mates and I have rolled up our shirtsleeves and plunged into the cool water to see if we could trap one of these golden fishes. Just along the other end of George Row was a local Smithy by the name of Crips. This particular building is still there. We used to go there to try and get the ball bearings we needed for our 'scooters'. I found out years later as I became more interested in local history, that the original

NEW CROSS SPEEDWAY

CRIPS OF DOCKHEAD – LAST SMITHY IN LONDON – FORMERLY A SAIL MAKERS business was that of a sailmaker to King George III's Naval ships and to this day the pole that the sailmaker would hang his 'sails' to dry can still be seen on the roof of the old smithy. More about this later.

Although it was very sad to us as kids whenever there was a funeral, it brings to mind the grand elegance of the hearse as these four or if you were too poor, only two, graceful black beauties, with their proud heads bearing the black plumes denoting death. One thing about the neighbours of our times, they would rally round anyone who was unfortunate, knocking on the doors of other neighbours and though they could ill afford it one was only too happy to give a couple of coppers to help some unfortunate friend. Because death was not a stranger to any family in those days, one would think 'if it happens to me I can rely on my neighbours for some support'. Not thinking in terms of money but real true neighbours would help out in any way they could. If they could not afford the few coppers then they would give up their time and help out by arranging the food on the return of the mourners. Oohs and Ahs would emanate from the lips of onlookers and one could tell the popularity of the dead person by how many neighbours or friends were waiting outside the door for the procession of mourners carrying wreaths or sprays and climbing into the waiting coach also they could tell how well off the family were by how many coaches one would have in attendance. Everything came to a standstill. Respect was shown by all persons along the route to the cemetery as kids we would run along side for as far as the end of the street looking in awe at the 'grown-ups' the men would doff their caps, some who knew the deceased would be seen to screw their cap in their hands. Women would stand and stare and openly cry as the hearse passed by. Alas will these ever return. I hope not for these were the days of real hardship and I hope never to be repeated, although at this present moment the trend is forever backward.

Christmas was the only time of the year when everything was O.K. Every kid that ever was had their own special wish or dream and it was at Christmas that friend or foe the time for forgetting was this special time of year. One would walk past all the shops gazing with wonder at the host of beautiful things that could be bought tinsel and ballooned decorated windows lit up with twinkling fairy lights. Wonders to behold with young eyes. As I look at the kids of today I often wonder if they realise the heritage that is theirs. I doubt very much if they can realise that what they take for granted today, that it was far beyond the reach of our delight to obtain such wonderful gifts that our own kids expect as their right today. Many is the time that I have secretly asked Father Christmas for a certain toy only to wake up on Christmas morning to find that He had not brought the gift I had set my young heart on. Still, we did not brood on it too long as there were compensations, and childlike we would become wrapped up in the Christmas festivities. One would find in the stocking, which was one of the sisters hung up the night before, oranges, nuts some picture puzzles that you had to break up first before you put it together again, a paper edition of snakes and ladders and another of ludo. In another packet would be some housey housey cards and a spinning top which would denote a number when it came to a stop and rest on it's side. Some dolly mixture a few nuts and a gazzoo. This was a musical toy that one could blow through and in a few moments you could be transported as the tunes of the day came forth. Lois Armstrong had nothing on us in our own world. Further down the stocking right in the toe, would be some bright new pennies. These would be held in hot hands till the 'gold' colour wore off or put away safe somewhere till it would maybe forgotten. We would fervently wish that it would snow on Christmas day and most times that I can remember it did. Although it did not remain white for long as with the traffic as it was it soon turned into slush and not a very nice colour. If we were up early in the morning and went out into the square or if you were lucky enough to live in a house, the backyard, and the only idea in ones mind was to build the biggest and best snowman. Snow still looks much nicer on the picture postcards. There was a small hill at the side of the George Pub in George Row, where we would make a slide and pretend we were the worlds greatest skier or tobogganist.

In the winter, it was increasingly difficult to warm the houses and on Saturdays us boys would go to where there were any road works to see if they had any 'tarry-logs'. These were wooden blocks that had been soaked in tar to preserve them on the roads and it would be a nice fire when one of these wooden blocks finally caught alight and burned brightly. Mind you, at first there was an almighty stink as the fumes of the tar were being burned out and many is the time a piece of stone grit exploded out from the fire grate to land anywhere on bare skin lord help you if it went into the eye. Nevertheless this item remained high on the list of priorities when it came to earning our picture money or money for sweets. Sometimes we would have to go as far away as China Hall in Rotherhithe. This was a council yard where they would take old tarry logs and store them up for re-use on the roads. These were sorted out and all those that weren't any good or were too split were then put onto a pile and sold for 2 pence a sack load. I have often seen old prams loaded up with as many sacks of these as one could push along in comfort by kids who would get a sack load for several neighbours, queueing up several times as we were limited to one sack each. This could take up a whole Saturday morning, which would mean that the early Saturday picture show was out for that day and maybe one could earn enough to go to the Matinee on the afternoon. Children were not allowed in the pictures unaccompanied in the evenings and at night you could see many an urchin-faced youngster, of which I was one, who would patiently wait for a single person going into the cinema and we would ask, "Take us in Mister" or Miss or Mrs. as the case may be. Very often the reply would be "No I can't it's time you were in bed", trudging home very disappointed if we could not get in by fair means or foul. There were doors round the side where some of the patrons would come out and not close the door properly whereby we would quickly 'bunk' in and very slowly crawl past the ushers in the aisle. This was a very happy pastime and one that we could boast about if successful. Looking back things seemed to be very poor. This was not the case inasmuch as we tended to make the best of anything and of course as children we did not have the worries that our parents had. Our worries were could we afford that 2oz of sweets that we fancied or to have a last fling with our ha'penny on a lucky dip. What a fantastic thing if we got the 'Star prize' of a quarter pound bar of chocolate. We could of course forfeit this for several other popular sweets such as bullseyes, brandy balls and naturally hundreds and thousands or even fairy sweets the very tiny globules of candy and they seemed to last forever. Another one of our wonderland journeys was to go 'down the blue'. This was a local market place in Southwark Park Road. There were loads of stalls with fruit and veg, wet fish with cockles, whelks and shrimps and winkles, toy stalls which was an Aladdins cave to young eyes. A special favourite was the biscuit stall. One could when it was packing up time, go to the stallholder and ask for biscuit crumbs. This was patiently wrapped up in a cone of newspaper and if you were lucky you could find yourself with several half biscuits with cream inside or once in a while you might get a chocolate covered piece. All in all it was a surprise packet. Wet the finger and dip it in the packet and out it would come with pieces of biscuit and you could lick it off. No thought of germs or the like entered the mind and we would make these crumbs last the whole night.

There was a shop in Abbey Street that we could take old jam

jars and get money on them. The pound jars would fetch a farthing each and the 2 pounders would be a ha'penny each. Sometimes the merry-go-round man would come round the streets with a portable merry-go-round on the back of a pony and cart and by turning a handle manually it would go round and round and for a jam jar you could get a ride on this magical machine. Or the rag and bone man would call round with his bell ringing out and calling out "any old rags, bottles or bones". This would be exchanged for anything he had on his cart at the time. Sometimes it would be a cup and saucer or a goldfish, according to how many rags you could give him. It wasn't until you were a lot older that you realised that it was quite a come-on.

  The Indian Toffee man was another delight that has no place in todays world. As it was very rare for a coloured person to be seen on the streets of London, we were always on the lookout for this particular interlude. The Indian toffee man would stand on the corner of the street and ringing a bell would cry out "Indian toffee good for your bellee". Then a mad rush would be made to get some of this special sweetmeat. The only resemblance to this today is the candy floss that one can buy at the seaside or at a fairground.

  The muffin man was another of these street hawkers. We would follow for quite a while the muffin man. Hoping against hope that he would drop one of his two trays that he carried on his head while ringing his bell. Then there were the Italian ice cream men. Now here was something that even the ice-cream vendors of today cannot produce. The flavours cannot be repeated no matter how much they try. The yellow ice which you could get with a piece of real lemon stuck in the top of an ice cream cone seem to last for quite a long time and if you wished for a mixed cornet for a ha'penny with lemon ice, vanilla cream and topped with strawberry. Such delicious memories.

  A trip to the Tower of London was a special treat and although it was not too far away, we could make a day of it. Afterwards we would stand on Tower Bridge and watch the boats on the river. Our favourite was watching the paddleboats that would take day trippers to Southend and then on to Clacton. I never forgot the time that my mother took me on one of these special trips. I had been unwell with whooping cough and it was suggested to my mother that this trip would be ideal for me. Walking round the decks during the trip so that I could get all the 'fresh air' that was to do me good so they said. I don't know if it really did but at least I am still alive to tell the tale. Another cure for this not very nice complaint was to take the children to the band-stand which was central in Southwark Park. Here every Sunday, there would be a band performance. It would be quite crowded. If you could afford it you could go inside the circled bandstand and sit on the folding chairs for a penny. Most people would stand against the railings and listen to the band. Marches, waltzes and when they played popular tunes you could hear them singing. It was an outing that we looked forward to. It was said that around the bandstand was four different types of air suitable for many chest complaints.

The Sunday that a lot of us looked forward to was the day that the local Catholic Church had their procession day. From early on in the morning people would begin to line the streets to get a good position to see the procession. The Catholic populace who had houses would decorate their windows with all their Holy Statues and various altar pieces. Their lace curtains making an altar cloth and they would compete with each other in the friendliest of way to see if they could 'outdo' each other. The lady whose window to me was always the best was Mrs. Large. She lived a few doors away from the George pub.

As the procession went past these window altars the owners would be standing at the side of it and the priest who led the processions would then come over to the 'altar' and then bless the house together

CATHOLIC PROCESSION — JAMAICA ROAD CHILDREN

CATHOLIC PROCESSION — JAMAICA ROAD
ADULTS

with the residents. These processions could take hours it seemed to us to go past. The young children would be dressed all in white with beautiful boquets and here again competition was rife to see who could make the prettiest basket for their daughters to carry in the procession. The pipers would follow the priests and then would follow the tableaus of the events leading up to the crucifixtion. After this would follow all the Saints and Martyrs the most popular being Joan of Arc.

It's funny, the kids of today are not as happy with their expensive toys as we were with our 'home-made' ones. The pride and joy one would have when a toy was made with our own ingenuity and it worked was a pleasure to behold.

Boat Race day was a day of rivalry between the blues of the area. We would go round to Teddy Carr's shop to get our rosettes and some of us never had the penny to pay for one we would rely on the generousity of Teddy if he had some over once the race had been finished and if it was the winner's colours it would be worn with pride.

There were the days we would go to St. James's Park. This park was only a small park which consisted of a few large flower beds surrounded by well rolled lawn. In the centre of this park was the inspiring church. One of the reasons we would go to this particular playground was to watch the 'posh' weddings. To see the limousines draw up outside the church and to take note of the guests and try to count the number of people that came to the wedding.

Another one of the favourite pastimes was the slide in the adjoining playground, this slide could be used no matter what the weather as it was under cover. You had to go in a side gate and there sitting in a hut would be the 'keeper of the slide'. She — or he — would then hand you a mat which you carried up a flight of stairs at the back. Place the mat on the top of the slide and get on it. It did not matter which way you sat on the mat. It could be on your belly or feet first or head first. The excitement was in sliding down and trying to beat your friends down and seeing how long it would take. You could always bet that some silly twit behind you would clomp you on the head when you reached the bottom and hadn't had time to get up. Never mind, we took it in good spirit.

My mother would take me to Tower Bridge Road where she did most of her shopping as this was one of our local market places. We would get a number 68 tram to the Trocette or outside of 'Trees' the jewellers, and along the side of the road from Grange Road to the Bricklayers Arms, would be the stalls which to us youngsters held all the delights we could wish for. Outside of Manzie's the eel and pie shop was a stall which had lots of trays on and we would stare in amazement at the size of these wriggling creatures. When a customer pointed to the eel they wanted you would then look on in horror as he grabbed the one that was chosen and with one mighty swipe of his large knife off would come the head of the eel. It was marvelous that the eel would go on wriggling even though it had lost it's head. The best part was when my mother would then take me into the Pie and Mash shop to taste the delights of their lovely thick pea soup. I have never since tasted this particular soup since the end of the war. Even though I have tried to capture the flavour it still did not taste the same as in the days of my youth. After this we would go to the bakers next door where my sister Lou worked and there we would get some cream cakes. This was luxury indeed for us as we could not really afford this but my sister would get some on discount. Home then to have a cup of tea with the cakes helping my mother with her shopping bags.

The season we liked best was in September. This was the hop-picking season and it was at this time of year that most of us in the area we lived in would pack up our bed clothes into a cart or pram and boxes piled on top would then push these contraptions up to the station.

SLIDE IN ST. JAME'S PARK — BERMONDSEY

Depending where one was going to would determine which station you would have to get to. I hoped it would be London Bridge. No such luck. I had to push it up to the Elephant and Castle station. There we would wait to get the hop-pickers special. This was nothing more than the early morning milk train, or post train. One mad rush to get our belongings onto the train and try to find a seat you'd be lucky. Off we go! When we got to the farm we children would then get out of our parents way while they went to the farmer's house to get the keys to the huts that they had been allocated. These were no more than a row of sheds. Inside the walls would be whitewashed and great big bundles of straw were placed there so that you could stuff it into clean fresh 'ticks'. These having come off the mattress at home. When this was done and the beds made, mother would then begin to hang some curtains around the hut to partition off and make some kind of bedroom as apart from the area where we would sit and eat. When the oil lamps were lit it was very cosy and warm inside the hut. Outside we would have a big bonfire going so that the cooking could be done. It was a very happy time sitting round the 'camp-fire' cooking jacket potatoes on the end of a long stick. Bedtime was early as we would have to rise early in the morning to get to the fields and pick a good position for the hop bins. These were made of wooden trestles which had sacking between the two ends and into this contraption we would pick the hops from the hop-vine. My father had a pole-pullers job. This meant that he would have a section of bins that he looked after. He would be issued with a long pole and if any of the vine was lodged on the upper strings he would have to use this pole to get it down and give it to the person whose row it was in. He also had to see that the floors of the row was picked clean of hops. This is where us kids came in, it was our job after the bins had moved up the row to pick all the loose hops from the ground, competition between the children would be to see how many

ROMAN QUINTAINE — OFFHAM, KENT

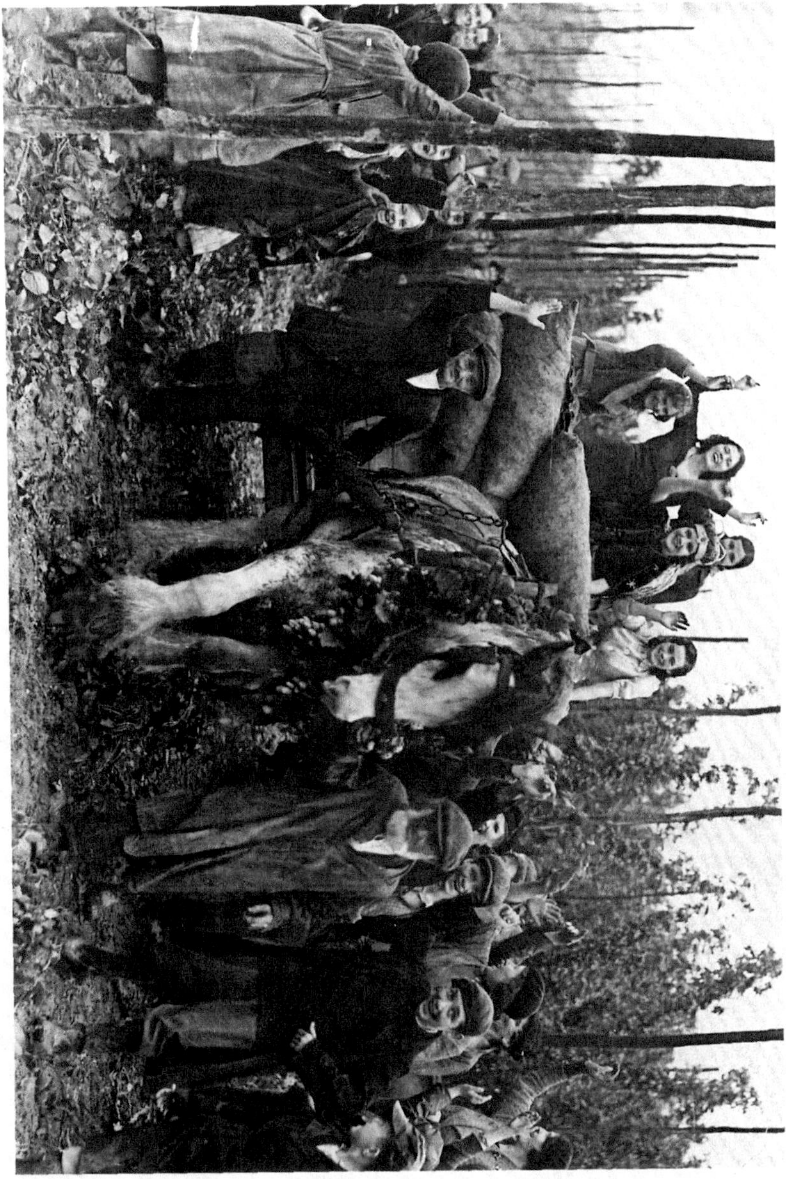

buckets we could fill. We would then get our 'pocket money' for this.

The place that was most popular with our family was a little spot in Kent that was called Offham. This place was particularly well known as it had on it's village green one of the very few Quintaines in this country. This farm was called May's farm.

The first day of picking was always jumpy as it was determined by how the measures were as to what the pay per bushel would be. It was hoped each year that the price would be better than the previous year. The number of measures a day was four and the farmers wife would do the measure and worked as hard as any man. Bending over the bin, push, push, push, in would go the hops and down would go the amount in the bin. We would stand around and peek into the bin and count how many bushels went into the sacks that the polepullers would hold for the measurer. My mums got more than your mum. No she ain't my mum picked more than your mum yesterday. This was the talk between us kids. We liked the time that the man with the horse and cart would come along to pick up the 'pockets' of hops and load them onto the cart. We would vie with each other to try and get the driver to let us have a go on the cart. If the farmer wasn't about then we might be lucky and get a ride back to the oast house. There we would help the driver unload the cart. On the second day of picking we would know what the pay per bushel would be. 3 pence a bushel. As one, the pickers would gather together and go to the farmhouse to see Mr. May the farmer. This was the pickers strike as they were not satisfied with the rate. After a while Mr. May would compromise with the pickers and back to work they would go. The 'strike' would not last more than a day. This would give the mums a bit more time to tidy up the hop huts or do a bit of shopping. No one was paid until the end of the hop picking but every Saturday afternoon there would be a long line of pickers outside the farmhouse lining up to get a 'sub'. This would be deducted at the end of the season. Sometimes if you had not picked good there would be very little to come at the end having subbed most of it to get food or go to the Red Lion at the Week-end.

To us kids this was a luvverly time. No school just going for walks and then doing some scrumping. You don't see the 'hopping apples' today. These were nearly as big as your head — or so it seemed to us — but I suppose these big apples are kept now for some other use. Shame! Mother used to wear a big pocket around her waist into which she would put the brass tally that would be given to her for every bushel she had taken from her bin. These would be given up to the farmer and the 'tally' put against her name. A man would come round the fields with a tray round his neck selling sweets or fruit "can we have some sweets mum go on lets have some" this was the cry from the kids. Sometimes it would be answered with "Get orf you bugger what jer think I'm made of. Money don't grow on the trees" this would be followed by yelps where some kid would get a swipe round the lughole. More often or not they would pay up to get us out of their way so that they could carry on picking.

I liked Saturdays best. This was the time that my dad would go into Maidstone where there was a pie shop that sold beautiful hot pies which had meat and potato in them.

Going home was one of the happiest and best parts of 'going hopping'. We would all gather at West Malling station and when we loaded up onto the train we would all start singing all the old songs. Us kids would have our own songs "When you go down hopping knock at number one, see old mother Riley etc..

When we arrived home a good bath was one of the first things that we did. "School on Monday for you me lad" my mother would say. "Can't I ave another week mum go on lets have another week".. I would cry. But mother was strong willed against my entreaties. But then it would be short lived as my mates would knock for me and out I would go to catch up on whats been happening in the neighbourhood during my absence.

Back to school! Ah me, what this conjures up for me was too much. The school that I went to was St. Joseph's Primary School in George Row. This was a Roman Catholic School and was run by the nuns of the convent Sisters of Mercy. To my small mind at this time there did not seem to be much mercy attached to them as invariably I would either have my ears boxed or tweaked or another of the sisters would flick you on the head with her silver whistle. I can assure them that this did hurt. I remember at one time we were given cards to put our pennies on. This was for the poor coloured children in Africa. We were told that we could put any name we chose on this card as a baptism name for one of these unfortunates. Now that they are over here, can we have our money back please!!! The only race relations board at this time was the street bookies that used to stand on the street corners or in the stairway of the blocks of flats and his 'runner' who would keep cavey on the look-out for the old 'bill' or if they knew beforehand that they would be nicked then they would get a 'ringer' who for a price would take the can-back for the bookie.

Old Wolseley buildings was a massive place. Built in Queen Victoria's time. It was a grim and forebidding structure, built like a prison, or so it seemed to me. As kids we would climb to the roof which was a flat affair and was used as a place for drying clothes for the residents of the flats. We could see for miles all over London from this spot and pick out all the places of interest. The Tower of London, the Monument at London Bridge on the other side you could see, on a clear day, Crystal Palace. The sight of the Thames on a sunny day, winding round like a silver ribbon snake with all the boats on it and the big cargo ships dotted along the wharves.

If we saw a sailor us kids would run up behind him to touch his collar for luck. What luck we would have today. Wow!! Sailors in our district was rare even if it was dockland. The crews from these ships were Merchant Men and were therefore not in uniform.

We all went swimming in Southwark Park Open Air Baths, one day and my mate Georgie said for a dare in front of the other boys, "I bet you would not dive off the top board", or the high diver as we called it, "No bloody **fear**" I replied, "Chicken" called the others. "O.K." I said climbing up the ladder steps to the high board. I heard myself saying "Tommy Ash you fool, you can't swim and you suffer from vertigo, what you doing up here". I edged to the end of the board and with my young life flashing before my eyes I half dived and half belly flopped to the water the backs of my legs hurt like hell. They dragged me out half drowned. Never again, no matter how like a chicken I seemed would I go through that performance again.

I was 12 years and 7 months old when we were listening to the radio and heard Neville Chamberlain announce to the world that we were at war with Germany. I went out to see my mates only to find that everyone had congregated at the schools where they were told all about evacuation plans. I did not go as I was not among those that were being evacuated to the country. Not for me leaving everything that I had ever known. It was not long before the first air raid siren went. Panic! Everyone said "quick, get down to the crypt". I thought to myself, why is it that the first thought in a persons head is to go to the nearest church. I have always wondered about this. Is it because of the inbred fear of God or is it the comfort of God. The priest told us all to kneel down and pray. It turned out to be a false alarm.

We made regular trips to the crypt as a safe place, taking our blankets and making sure of our spaces for the family. After a time when the war didn't seem to be doing anything in London, we gave up our place down the crypt and stayed at home. Not for long though, as we were to experience the most concentrated air raids of the war, day and night bombing. Dog fights in the air and this period was to be history in the making for it was known now as the 'Battle of Britain' and the heroic defence of our fighter pilots historically known as 'the few' by our most famous of Prime Ministers, Winston Churchill who made his most rhetoric speech about our pilots. His vehement speeches against Hitler or in Winnie's terms 'Mr. Schicklegruber' was to inspire the whole nation and when visiting the cinema we would wait for the News Reel to come on and when Churchill appeared on the screen with his famous 'V' for victory sign such cheers would resound that it was quite deafening. The same happened whenever any happening of our 'boys' in the army, navy or air force came on the screen. I was one of the many who shouted as loud as I could.

  The night that the Luftwaffe made their first attack on dockland was horrifying. The old fire of London in 1666 was nothing compared to this if the books I read about the Fire of London was anything to go by. The brilliance of the red sky over the whole of the dock area and in the city of London was a sight that I would not like to witness again. The clanging of the fire engines and the alarm of the ambulances made deafening noises. The Pom Pom guns up and down the railway lines was useless against these fast in and out bomb dropping enemies. A small respite in the morning as Londoners tried desperately to carry on as normal, many doing their business in the streets outside their place of employment. Stout hearted, they called us. It reminds me of the song we sang at school, Hearts of oak are our ships, etc...

  We started to go to one of the railway arches which had been turned into Air Raid Shelters. Queueing up at four o'clock in the afternoon for my mother with bundles of blankets and things that one might need during the long nights vigil. Getting spaces for the family, not only

STAINER STREET ARCH – TOOLEY STREET
60 KILLED & OVER 100 INJURED DURING WORLD WAR II

Miss Florence Donovan

dad and mum but my married sisters with their children. Some of my sisters had been evacuated but had returned to London. We were staying in Stainer Street arch at nights when my dad said that we would go to London Bridge tube station and get bunks there. This seemed like heaven to us as we were fed up with lying on the hard ground. Funny thing though, we went to the tube and soon after this on one night raid, Stainer Street arch had a direct hit with a bomb. There were many killed in this arch and a lot more that were injured. I shall never forget my feelings when I heard about it. After a while we got used to hearing the thud, thud, thud of the bombs and the pom pom pom of the guns. To overcome our fears singing could be heard and many is the time someone would get up and give a turn either by singing or on a musical instrument. At last, it was clear that the war was not going to be won overnight and that we really did have a long fight on our hands, the people turned their hands to make things in the shelters as comfortable as possible. A canteen was set up at night, hot tea, coffee, of sorts, soft drinks where possible, and sandwiches I don't know where it all came from as I knew that rationing was very tight. I supposed that the women had got some sort of extras from the Ministry of Food. It could also be that someone was acquainted with the other people i.e. black market. Still, no questions asked, no lies told. We were happy to accept small comforts no matter where it came from.

  When queueing up for our places in the tube, I would get up in the morning and straight away go outside and start to queue up for the nightime. My mother would send along to me my food from home. I would then be joined by another member of my family who would then take over whilst I went home to have a clean up and change my clothes. I would eat my food while sitting on the kerbstones along side of the road. I remember one morning waking up to be told that we would have to walk along the railway lines as we could not go out the normal way because a parachute mine was hanging on one of the signals over our heads. Being young and foolish us kids saw no danger and went up top, what a sight we saw the firemen fighting a fire in the hop warehouses in Snowsfield, nearby Guy's Hospital had got a direct hit you could still hear the bombs exploding. At night it was a sight to see the searchlights picking out the offending areoplane then all hell was let loose.

I will always remember when I left St. Joseph's Primary School and had my first encounter with a teacher at the Secondary School called 'Moggy Donovan'. She used to play the piano, especially at Prayer time. Being a Catholic School the first thing we had to do on entering the hall was to dip your finger in the Holy Water, make the sign of the cross, genuflect before the altar and then take your place in the line up. I hated this part, I don't know why even now. Moggy would play the hymns, she was a right old so and so and if you were late she would say "Right, off you go to see Mr. Cottrell", he being the head master.

I was always a bit of a dunce at school and never really got on with the lessons. I was forever looking over the shoulder of the boy next to me to try and get the answers. Sometimes the twit sitting next to me would twig what I was doing and cover up so that I could not see. The teacher would call me out in front of the class and the humiliation of this is with me to this day. As you can see, I never really liked school and when the war came and the school was evacuated I never returned to school.

I can't help thinking of the butchers shop at Shad Thames. My mother used to send me there to get 4 farthing faggots and half a dozen eggs. This princely meal would cost about 6 pence. Such delights of this shop faggots and pease pudding or red hot saveloys all juicy makes your mouth water to think about it.

Although the times were hard we never really went hungry all us boys would go to either Shad Thames or Butlers Wharf where the dockers would throw away all the spunky oranges. They would open the gates when we came along and let us go and sort through them to try and get the better ones. Sure enough we would get quite a few. They would of course throw out some good oranges in amongst them. We would also go along to the Borough Market where we would glean some potatoes or apples which would fall from the lorries when being unloaded.

    Dockhead had quite a sharp bend by the 'Sugar Loaf' pub and many's the time when a lorry came round this bend and would shoot it's load onto the pavement outside Charlie Mellish's the paper shop. When this happened, especially if it was tins of corned beef, tomatoes or the like, we would scramble to see how much we could load up. There was a mad rush, not only the kids but the women as well, loading up their prams so that it would be hard to see the baby inside. Of course when the cops came along everyone would disappear and the driver of the lorry would be looking the other way or trying to get some of the passing men to help him load his lorry again.

    On the corner of Abbey Street there used to be an old coffee stall which stood outside the old Christ Church. There you could get a nice cup of tea and a hot pie which would be cut in quarters and some brown sauce poured on top. This made a very nice stop up meal and cost only 3 pence. There used to be another man who would sell baked jacket potatoes. This was a special treat for us and at a halfpenny each, worth its weight in gold for it's mouthwatering delight. On a cold winters night you could stand around his fire which was like a barrel of an old steam engine on which there were spikes that would pierce the potatoes and bent over the fire to roast. Another juicy morsel that another bloke would carry round in a basket would be the pigs trotters these would last a long time and would provide our supper on a

Saturday night.

I shall never forget the time when one of my mates went to the local undertakers (Albins) and told him that his mum had sent him to ask Mr. Albin to come around his house in Little Copperfield as his uncle Dickie had passed on. When Mr. Albin knocked on the door, it was answered by my mates uncle Dick who went quite pale when Mr. Albin said "I have come to measure Mr. .... They do say that the shock was too much even for the undertaker.

Going to the cinema cost only tuppence and after a night at the flicks you could go along to the fish and chip shop and get tuppenny-ha'penny piece of fish and a ha'porth of chips. To make the weight up you could ask for some crackling. You would get quite a lot of this crackling for a ha'penny if you could not afford to buy the full fish and chip supper. We would walk along the street with these steaming bits of batter and really enjoy ourselves.

On the corner of Thurland Road opposite St. James's church was the local Pawn Shop. This shop did a roaring trade on a Monday morning. You could see them lining up all the way round the corner and as soon as 'Uncle' opened up there would be a mad rush to get in. Mostly bundles of newly washed bed linen and the old mans weekend suit and shoes well polished. This would get the rent money and Monday's dinner. Saturday morning there would be another long queue to redeem the pledges. Sometimes old 'Uncle' would say "Take care of them or else I will have to dock the money on Monday". Shoes were the hardest to pawn because they would show the wear. No matter how much spit and polish went on them. Even the soles would be washed and polished so that when taking it in on Monday morning you would hear the ladies say,. "'e never even wore them but I'ado take 'em out satday just in case 'e wanted to go out". Nevertheless, Uncle would invariably dock so much every week until he would not even

F.A.ALBIN.
UNDERTAKER
Funeral F.A.ALBIN Furnisher
EMBALMING
CREMATIONS
FUNERAL
FURNISHER

PAGES WALK

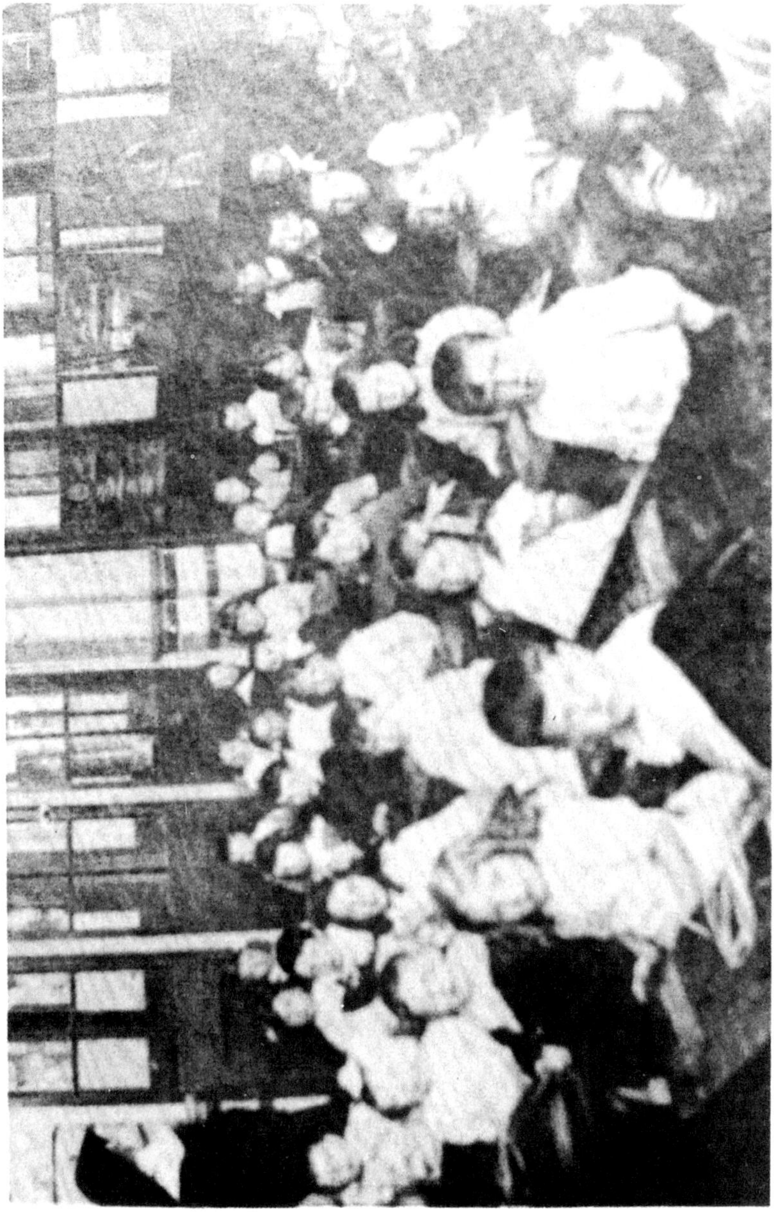

ST. JAMES CHURCH BERMONDSEY
— COMMEMORATING THE BATTLE OF WATERLOO

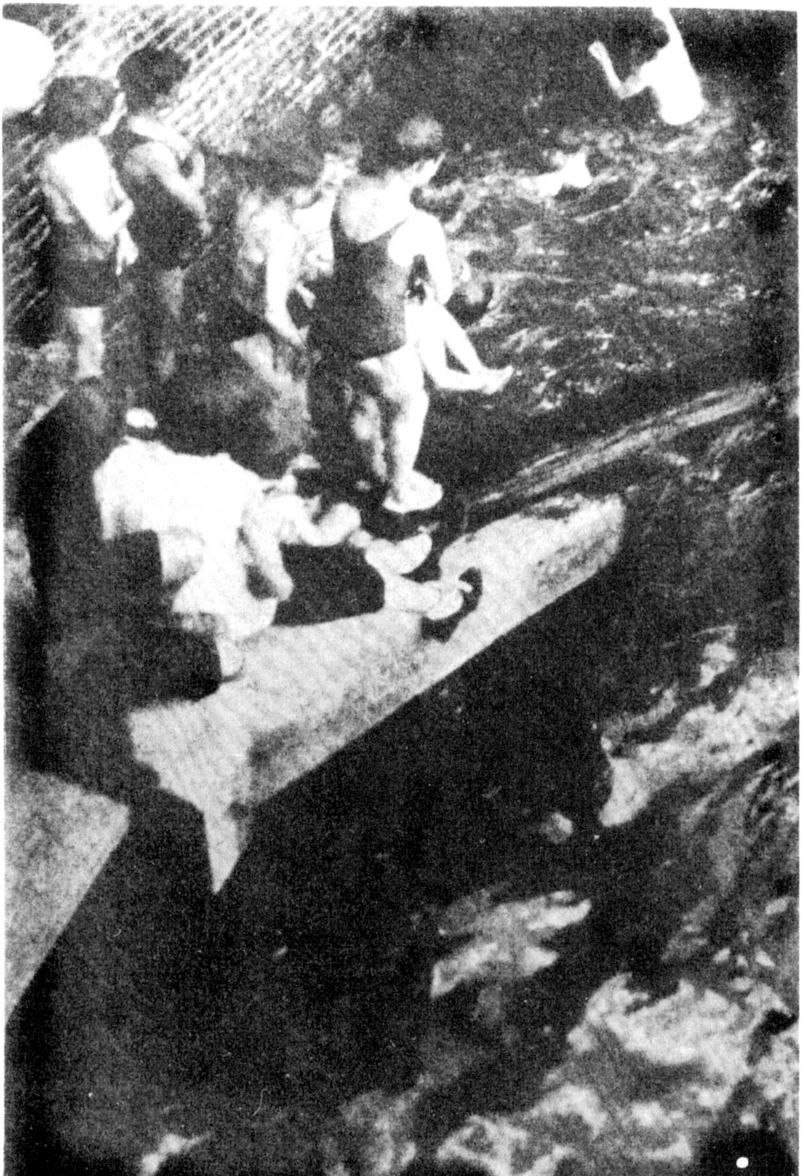

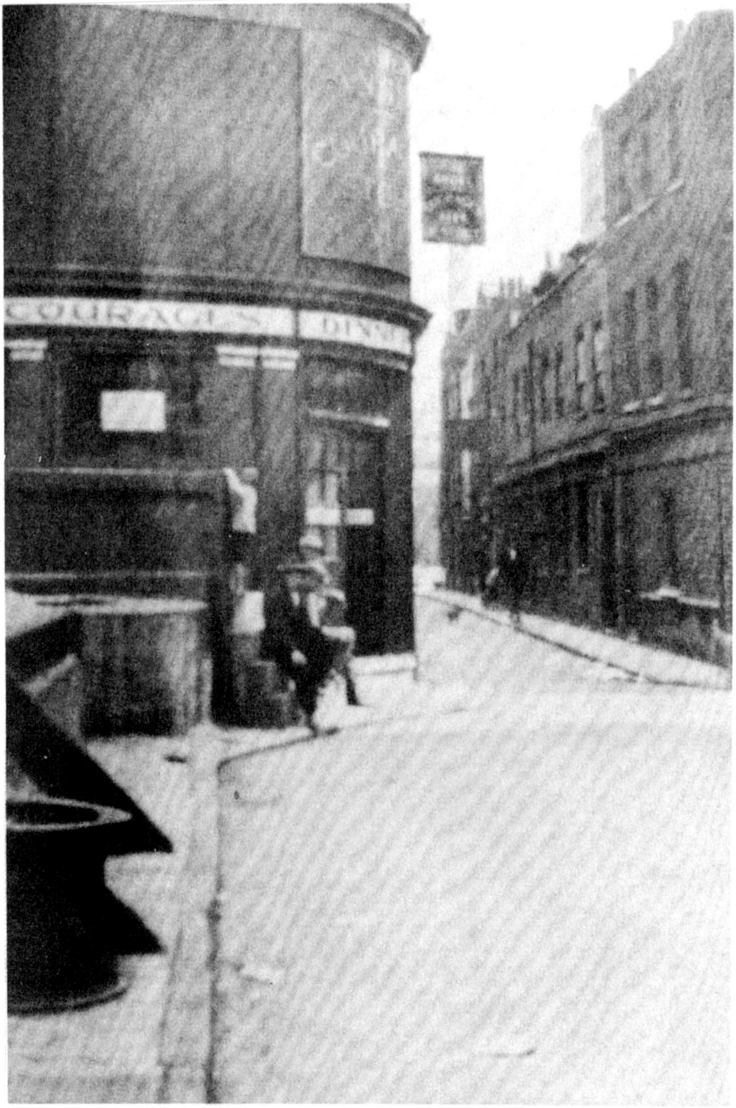

accept them for a pledge. Sometimes, if you could not afford to redeem the pledge you would ask 'Uncle' to renew the interest only. Pawn tickets would last for six months on jewellery and 1 year on clobber. I knew a woman, an aunt of a friend, who had a purse full of pawn tickets, enough to play cards with and each month she would sort out all those that were up for renewal or any that 'just had to be got out' only to be pawned again the following week. Sometimes for more than it was originally in. 'Uncle' would try to come the old acid when renewing a pledge by saying the item was worth less but back would come the answer that 'I only got it out on Friday and it was in for a lot more than that'. One would try not to antagonise him too much just in case he refused to take the pledge at all or say go somewhere else, knowing full well that you couldn't as the next nearest pawn shop was streets away and you had to be back in time for the landlord.

Many a time we would cadge a penny from one of our parents and if lucky we would go along to the oil shop in Dockhead and buy a fishing net and off we'd go with a jam jar tied with a piece of string around the neck so that we could carry it easy. Our favourite place to fish was East Lane Pier. This was just some wooden steps leading down to the waterside. After the tide had gone out these steps were very slippery and green slime on the edges. We had to be careful so off would come our shoes and socks and rolling up our trouser legs so as not to get them wet, we would go to the rivers edge and try to catch a fish. All we landed up with was a few sticklebacks. Never mind, we were happy just to get anything and we would tell stories of how big our 'catch' was and always the fisherman's tale of the one that got away.

One time we were fishing where we were not supposed to be and a copper came and caught us. You never saw such speed as we kids ran down the street in our bare feet up along Cherry Garden pier. I must say that the water of the river in those days was a darn sight cleaner than it is today. At least you could see through the water at low tide and see the bottom.

Charlie Mellish's the paper shop was a gathering place for me and my mates as we got our favourite comics there. The Beano, Dandy, Hotspur. Desperate Dan was a joy to us and the antics of Lord Snooty kept us amused. The Hotspur with it's dearth of stories about sport was one we all really enjoyed. We would also get our bullseyes, sherbet dabs or gob-stoppers. These would be special for us — the gobstoppers — we would see whose stopper would last the longest. Such joy! In Pavey's, next to the Sugar Loaf we could buy Fruit Ice Cubes for a farthing each. Sucking these fruit ices we would go into the back of the shop where there were pinball machines. Out would come the 'magic' piece of film that one of us always carried, and placing this piece of celluloid over the 'penny hole' we could get a free go. O.K. Whose going first, would be the cry. "Mee, mee" would come the cry from all of the others. Terry, my best mate would say "I'm the leader my turn first". "O.K. I'm next". In the end we would toss for who would go next. Knowing my luck I would be last.

'Nitty Norah' what thoughts this name would conjure up as we trooped into our classrooms in the morning. This was a nickname given to the visiting nurse who would grab hold of your hair and with several swift movements of the head would determine whether or not it was your turn to go to the delousing centre round the Neckinger. It was shameful in front of the whole school if you were one of the unfortunate ones. Lucky enough my mother was very good at keeping our heads clean. I can remember her telling the tale of one day when my eldest sister came home from school with a card telling her that she had to go and have her hair done. This infuriated my mother so much that she went to the school and in front of the classroom practically stripped my sister of every stitch of clothing shouting at the poor frightened nun.

My mother received a note of apology from the nurse who stated it was done in error as the girl who was to have her hair done gave the wrong name.

Bermondsey, my home town, I have lived there all my life the only times that I went out of the Borough was as I have told it during the hop-picking season or on day trips to the sea-side. It has altered so much that a lot of it's character is missing but if one looks around you can still see quite a bit of that which gave Bermondsey it's name.

One of the most famous women of Bermondsey was the famous or infamous Joanna Southcott who lived in a house on the corner of Jamaica Road and Abbey Street.

It was claimed that this fanatical person possessed an uncanny power over the people and she claimed to be a second Virgin Mary in that she had become pregnant by a miraculous conception and that she was expecting a second Jesus. The people of Bermondsey even went to the length of providing a silver cradle and a place of worship. She would often be seen addressing crowds of people outside the old drill hall.

'Oh ever thus from childhood's hour, I've seen my fondest hopes decay; I never loved a tree or flower but was the first to fade away''. How this old poem brings memories of the walks in the flower garden in Southwark Park on a bright summer's day. The beautiful roses in the popular Rose Garden surrounding the lake was another world. One could walk in that delicious atmosphere and forget that you were in the middle of such a drab location. The magnificent white swans that we would save our crusts for and faithfully feed them along with various ducks that swam in the wake of the graceful swans. Over on the other side of the park was the greens. On Sundays you would find the older type male gently putting the golf ball around the small course. Further along was the bowling green where the elderly gentlemen and their wives would gently tease the woods up the velvet-like green. In the cage, this was a covered in structure so that the balls would not go over the top and hit passers by, in summer the game of cricket in winter football. Competition cricket was played in the 'Oval'. It is said that the oval was exactly 1 mile in circumference and you could often see athletic persons doing their routine early in the morning around the oval. At the park gates just inside of Gomm Road were the hothouses. These were opened to the public on Sundays and passed many a pleasant hour or two just walking around the several greenhouses that housed the exotic plants with all the fantasies of the tropics one would imagine.

When all the neighbours left Oxley Street we would climb over the walls and into the houses we would go to see what we could find. Sometimes you would find parts of a tin toy train set or other broken toys. We would try to fix them so that they could work after a fashion. One time when we were there the local 'bobby' came along and saw us. I jumped over the fence but he caught me. When he took me home and asked my mother "Is this your boy?" my mother said "Yes", "Well, if I catch 'im again, I'll run 'im in". The police were a lot more tolerant then than they are now. They would rather give you a caution than go through the rigmarole of taking you to court. Mind you, this was only for very slight misdemeanors.

Dockhead, the parish where I lived has had many historic events. In 1849 – 1854 cholera came to Dockhead and over 200 people succumbed to this disease. There were 19 cases reported in one house alone. Smallpox was another of those diseases that seemed to thrive in the sort of district that has been recorded in the old graveyards that we used to see. All of these have disappeared during the war and due to the re-organisation of the Borough.

Dockhead was mainly made up of Irish immigrants. These illiterate people earned a meagre living on the waterside trying to get a days work on the wharves or as labourers on the roads and some became costermongers.

It was after the potato famine in Ireland that the poor people of Ireland emmigrated to England and on to London where they settled in various Boroughs. A good many of them settled in Dockhead and made a small tight colony of Irish. These people were resented by the Protestants of the parish because they did not understand the way the Catholic people lived. The parish church for the Catholic contingency was the Holy Trinity Church. This was designed by Augustus Pugin, a very famous architect of the day, in 1834 as was first used by the parishioners the following year, by the Rev. Dr. Branston. This was a typically Pugin church who followed the Gothic style and this church settled the needs of the Roman Catholic population of the parish.

Further along Parkers Row on the corner of Abbey Street was the parish church of the Protestants named Christ Church. This was a Romanesque in design but not up to the standard of Trinity Church.

Trinity Church was commissioned by the Baroness Montesquieu and was quite well supported by it's parishioners. It provided a lot of relief through the St. Vincent de Paul funds, this was part of the Sunday collections which was divided up for several charities as well as paying for the duties of the priests.

Another of the local churches which I have already mentioned was St. James Church. This was a more select church and was a Protestant church. It was also one of the Waterloo churches built to commemorate the battle of Waterloo. It is said that the bells of the church were made out of the cannons that were captured at Waterloo.

On Sundays you would see the carriages of the select people, mainly old sea captains and merchants of the district who lived in the better quality houses of the district. These houses were Georgian Style and to the poorer people they appeared to be mansions compared to the back to back terrace houses that abounded in the area. These are the sort of people who attended St. James for Sunday services and many of them are to this day buried in the churchyard, where the old tombstones can be seen. In the church there was always a pair of extending tongs and these were known as dog catchers. If a stray dog came into the church the verger would catch them with these tongs and put them outside.

Jacobs Island — This was the area that ran from Jacob Street up to Mill Street at the end of which was a wooden bridge leading to 'Jacobs Island'. This was the spot that gave Charles Dickens his background for his book Oliver Twist and the Fagins hovel. It was after visiting the district and seeing how the poor lived that gave him the idea.

Hickman's Folly — This was a street that was named after a certain Mr. Hickman who opened a fair on this site in the 18th century and proved to be a flop. This street ran from George Row to just past the 'Sugar Loaf' public house and up past Jacob's Biscuit factory and on to the corner of Devon Mansions.

On the corner of Hickman's Folly there used to be the local barbers shop with a pole outside that would denote that he was also the local physician he was also a dentist. People who were brave enough to come forward to have a tooth extracted would be given gin, which was quite plentiful, and with the screwing contraption would extract the offending tooth. He would have coloured water in glass bottles in his window showing that he also dispensed his own medicines. Inside he would have apples with string going through them which would then be hung up, this would be given to patients who had fever.

The Ship Aground — This pub was named after an old inn that was owned by a retired sea captain — Thomas Watkins. When the old sailing ships came into the wharves or docks, they used to come and visit their old friend who would always welcome them aboard as he

The "Hanover Arms," Neckinger.

THE SHIP AGROUND

classed his inn as a 'ship aground'.

Abbey Street — This was of course named because of Bermondsey Abbey which was there hundreds of years ago. The abbey was famous in that it was a resting place for pilgrims who were making their way to Canterbury. It was also the place where the first Queen Elizabeth was virtually a prisoner before she was to become Queen of England.

After the dissolution of the Abbey there were many Catholic churches which were pulled down. Those that were left standing were converted to the Protestant faith. The Catholic faith was forbidden and a law against the Mass being said or sung brought dire rewards. Churches were desecrated and set fire to and Catholics were called upon to take an oath declaring their alleigance to the Queen and to refuse to follow the dictates of the Pope in Rome. No Catholic was allowed to travel more than 5 miles from their home and were not permitted to reside within 10 miles of Westminster. Catholics were also forbidden to enrol for army or navy service. Any Catholic priest caught saying Mass was either imprisoned or put to death.

The sufferings of the Catholics in Bermondsey were very severe and lasted for many years. It was not until 1778 that saw the end of the persecution. The Relief Act came upon the scene which gave the Catholics the right to follow their religion and 'Mass Houses' with their 'Priest Holes' were no longer needed and were replaced by Chapels and on the 2nd Relief Act in 1791 the Catholic churches sprung up again and were tolerated a bit more.

In 1773 there was one of these Chapels built in Flockton Street and was attended by the Irish workers who laboured on the waterside in the tanneries and other work in the area. The first site for a Chapel was built on the site which would later become known as East Lane School. In the register of Births and Marriages the priests would not sign their names to these documents for fear that they would be informed upon for the £100 reward which the informer would receive.

The Protestants detested the Repeal Act and on Friday 2nd of June 1780 they sent a petition to Parliament but it was rejected.

Violence was no stranger to Bermondsey. The latter part of the 18th century the Chapel in Flockton Street and the house of one named Mr. French were burned to the ground by the Protestants. Other houses were also 'marked out'.

There was great rivallry between the Protestants and the Roman Catholics to provide schools for the children of the district. The Catholic priests knew that if the children went to a school run by Protestants that they would soon lose sight of their faith and this they did not want. So with this in mind the priests went to their parishioners homes to collect what little they could towards building a Catholic school. Father Broderick started an outdoor collection in 1799. Being populated by the Irish Catholics the priests could speak Irish as well as English. The number of Catholic people in the parish swelled to 3,000 but because work was not plentiful and what with the living conditions being what they were life in the parish was not very acceptable and got the nickname of being an 'Irish Rookery'. The old Chapel in Flockton Street was so small only accommodating 400 so at every Mass it was full to overflowing.

One day in 1831, Father Peter Butler was asked to appear before Bishop Bramston when the Bishop asked Father Butler if he would undertake to build a new church in Dockhead. His reply to the Bishop was "Here I am, send me and I will do your bidding". He was appointed to the job of getting started with the plans for the building of what was to be the Holy Trinity Church of Dockhead.

Not getting very far where money was concerned in building the church he was then visited by the Baroness de Montesquieu who was appalled at the conditions of the parish. She then promised to help in any way she could to see that the Bishop's promise of a new church for Father Butler was fulfilled by donating money towards the building of the Church. It was with this aid that Pugin was approached to design the church then the building was soon underway.

A room was hired in the Star public house and there every Sunday the congregation would troop in and hand over what little money they could afford. There was a vacant plot of land that was being put up for sale in Parkers Row, Dockhead and with the money that was collected from the people of the parish it was purchased for the new church.

The foundation stone of the new church was laid on the 3rd August 1834 and was completed in 1835. On the 25th June of the same year all the Catholics of the parish gathered at the old Chapel in Flockton Street and a procession was made to the new church led by Father Butler.

After this the next thing was to get the schools under way. One school for the girls and one for the boys of the parish. Money was still very scarce but with perseverance against adversity these buildings were completed.

The Convent of the Sisters of Mercy was built in the same style as the church and Lady Barbara contributed £1,000 towards the building of this which in those days was quite a lot of money. The Convent was built on the site of what used to be a local tannery. Bermondsey at this time was known as the Land of Leather.

The parish of Dockhead became fairly well known because of the church and was administrated by the local priests. The funds were enriched by donations from the parishioners and by some influential people locally. It was to this parish that the Bishop of the diocese would look forward to generous donations for any charitable please.

My father was a Catholic and my mother was of Protestant faith and when they got married the priest would visit them and try to convert my mother adding that according to the Catholic church they were not married in the sight of God. My paternal grandmother would have nothing to do with my mother and likewise my maternal grandmother would not have much to do with my father although unlike my fathers mother she would treat him the same as her daughter when they visited but my fathers mother was quite different and I have often heard my mother say that when she visited her with the children she would offer a dinner to my father but not to her or the children. My father would accept the food and offer some to my mother who would refuse to eat it. This shows to what extent the then animosity towards each other the different religions went. Needless to say my mother did become converted to the Catholic faith sometime later on.

I was born in 'Dickens land' so named because of it's association with the writer Charles Dickens. All the buildings around our way had some connection with the characters from his books. The entire estate was known as Dickens Estate. There was Wade House, Bardell, Copperfield, Tupman, Tapley, Nickleby, Pickwick, Brownlow, Fleming, Rudge, Havisham, Micawber,etc. I could go on and on.

It was actually in Virginia Row that I was born in a two up and two down terraced house. My grandmother delivered me after asking the doctor to go for a walk because he was not helping my mother along with the birth. By the time he had finished his smoke I was born washed and wrapped up. I was about 3 years old when we had to go from our house. I can always remember the backyard of the house as we kept a nanny goat out there and one day my brother decided he didn't like the colour of the goat and painted it green. My old man didn't half belt him one as he told him that I was the one who did it. We moved around the corner into the new flats that we had watched being built. This was Copperfield House. I remained there until 1958.

I remember the lamplighter who used to come around the streets lighting up the street lamps with his long pole that had a taper inside of the stick. We would follow him for what seemed like miles watching to see if he missed one.

The people were very trustworthy in those days, as you could see sticking out from many a door or letterbox a piece of string which you pulled to open the door and it is said that one never bolted or locked their doors at night. I suppose that everyone was in the same boat in those days and did not have anything of value worth pinching. I am certain you could do nothing like that today.

In 1911 before the first world war, the Salvation Army which was situated in Spa Road, used to employ on average 400 - 500 casual workers for paper sorting. The men were mainly destitute or were out of work. During the first week they were given food and lodging and in the second week they would be given a princely sum of sixpence to help them. Some of them who had initiative, would, if they worked hard, earn as much as 4 or 5 shillings. An officer in charge was asked by a well known writer, Rider Haggard, what he had to say to the charge of sweated labour and his reply was "no, these men were only drunkards or unskilled men who had no value on the work market".

The Sally Army as it was called, collected waste material from warehouses piling it up on horsedrawn carts with Salvation Army in white on a red background, the men they employed would then sort it out into different grades baling them into the hydraulic balers ready to be sold to the paper merchants at a fair profit. Furniture, bric a brac was collected also and sold for a few pence to the poor of the area and the money gained was spent to upkeep the lodging house. It still goes on today.

Spa Road was named after Mr. Keyse, Spa Gardens, which was famous for its waters and was visited by many famous people one being the noted engraver William Hogarth and many a time, to celebrate royal occasions, he would have military bands and fireworks. The price at the time was too much for the poor but for the people he catered for were the better class in the borough such as the merchants and the tannery owners and their families. The waters were so rich in minerals that it was said that George III took them quite regularly.

Spa Road was the site for the Town Hall of Bermondsey which is still there and the Public Lending Library designed by Mr. John Frowde which housed at one time, the finest collection of the history of the borough from medieval times when Bermondsey Abbey and the surrounding district was marsh land to the 2nd World War. This was a happy hunting ground for students of local history. Many of these books have left Bermondsey and are housed in the Newington Library which now comes in the bounds of Southwark Borough, which I think is a shame.

Cockney, a word that describes people from certain areas of London, was an old name of a person who lived in London. It was said that a Londoner being in the country and hearing a horse neigh said "How that horse laughs". A yokel standing nearby corrected him and said that the word was neighing. The next morning the Londoner on hearing the cock crow said, and to show that he was no fool, "How that cock neighs". This is just a silly fable that countryfolk like to tell about the ignorance of Londoners of the time. It is also applied to any person living within the sound of the Bow Bells. My own opinion is that in the old days when cockfighting was around and being a very proud bird, a working class man was proud and respected by his fellowman who would cry out a greeting to one another "Wotcher cock", this I presume could have slurred into the word cockney.

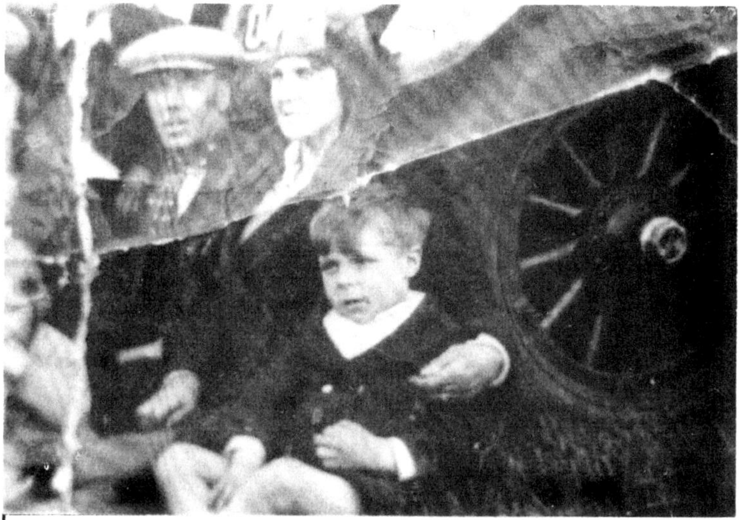

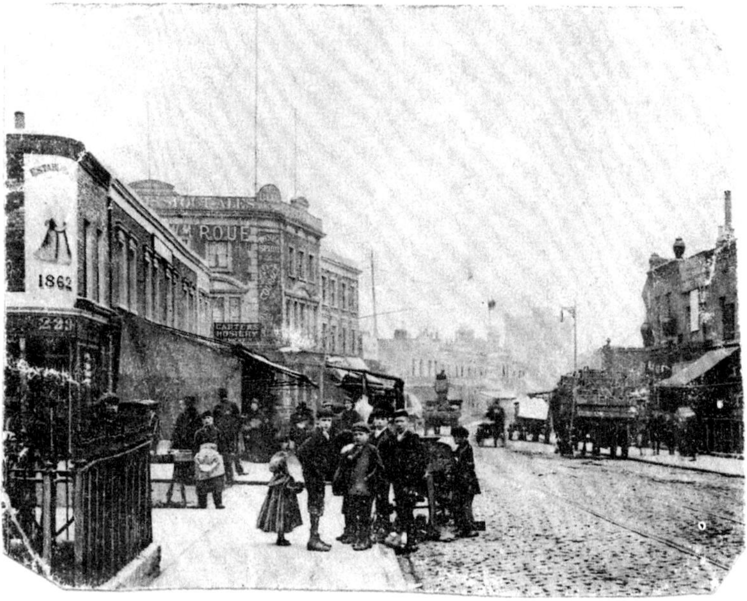
1862
CARTERS HOSIERY

Canon Murnane

OLD ENTRANCE TO SURREY DOCKS

GREENLAND YARD – SITE OF THE OLD HOWLAND DOCK

Among my collections which I bought at the Bermondsey Market some years ago are some old land deeds. These describe the rents of houses in Dog Street which was later to become known as Dock Street. Peppercorn rent was valued at one red rose a year. Looking at these deeds I sometimes wonder whether the Isle of Dogs was corrupted from the Isle of Docks.

I never thought I would see the day when the docks would be closed down but alas this is just the case.

Surrey Docks, one of the oldest docks in London, has now been filled in. It was first known as the Great Howland Wet Dock and was owned by Mrs. Howland, later it was to become Greenland Dock for use in the whaling industry.

Here they employed men to boil the blubber from the whales for use in extracting oil for lighting and also for the perfume industry. When the docks closed it was decided in the year 1807 to re-open the docks renaming it The Surrey Commercial Docks. It was not very big at that time about 300 odd acres. Timber was left in the Lavender Yard in the water to season till it was wanted by the merchants. Close to Greenland Dock in Plough Road, was Dudmans or what it is now called Deadmans Dock. This was a small dock built by Mr. Dudman and not as dockers would have you to believe that a deadman was found there when the navvies were building the dock.

Further along from this dock was Convoys which at one time was an old victualling yard. This once belonged to the Navy and it was from here that Captain Cook left by sail on some of his voyages. It took him two weeks to sail from here to Plymouth.

Nearby is one of the oldest churches, St. Nicholas, in South London. There is no record of when this was built but it was proved by grant by the Countess Juliana de Vere to the religious order of Premonstratensians or White Canons. The 12th century parts were rebuilt again and again by the parishioners and the only original parts left is the tall tower which was used in the time of the first Queen Elizabeth as a beacon where a fire was lit in a brazier on top of the tower to guide ships in bad weather into the docks. It is said that two naval officers who are buried here were hanged for fleeing from the enemy during battle. To this day there can be seen two gloomy skulls on either side of the gates.

The last person to die from the plague in 1665 is buried in St. Marychurch in Rotherhithe. I have seen the register of births, deaths and marriages which was kindly shown to me by the vicar of St. Marychurch, dating back to the time of the plague.

It was from this waterside spot that the famous ship the Mayflower began its long and gruelling journey to the New World. Although the ship started from this spot in Rotherhithe, the passengers who did not fancy the three week journey by sea to Plymouth, especially the English Channel, travelled overland to Plymouth to await the ship and embark from there.

THE PLAGUE GATES OF ST. NICHOLAS CHURCH DEPTFORD

THE MAYFLOWER, ROTHERITHE

ST. MARYCHURCH ROTHERHITHE

OLD WATCH HOUSE OUTSIDE CEMETERY TO STOP BODY SNATCHERS

CHAPTER 2

When I first entered the docks in 1960, I soon found that it was not all jam and honey. You had to go up and down the wharves to try and get a days work. I used to go around with my brother Joe. We would go out at six thirty every day and go to Cherry Garden Pier and there we would meet up with several other dockers and because we were the 'early people' we soon became known as the 'Dawn Patrol'.

To the right of the pier we could see Brandrams Wharf where we usually 'shaped' on average twice a week. The two boats were the Rini and the Zeehound. These ships were owned by a Dutch family and they carried strawboards. Working on these boats would get us right out of pawn if the week proved to be a bad one.

To the left of the pier was Chambers Wharf, and we could tell if the Stroom boats were in — or the 'A' boat. This was so named because of the big 'A' on the side of its funnel.

Further down from Brandrams Wharf, we could see Bellamy's which was built by the French prisoners during the Napoleonic war. The strange thing about the docks were the nicknames that some of the men acquired. At Brandrams for instance, one man was called the 'Bear' because of the way he used to growl. Another was called 'The Terrible Turk' and of course there was 'Home Grown' because of his habit of saying "a luvverly bit of 'ome grown". There were the men known as 'The Green Jackets' these were a group of men who were always dressed in combat jackets acquired from the Army & Navy Surplus Stores.

At Deadmans Dock, where the stone boats used to come in, and the work was mainly done by 'grabs' and the only work done by the men was the trimming, these were known as 'Dads Army'. Another gang was called 'Hogan's Heroes' and our own gang when we worked on the strawboards became known as 'The Cardboard Cavaliers'. When working at Chambers there was one guy that was called 'Saucebottle' as the saying went 'you could see a better pair of shoulders on a sauce bottle'.

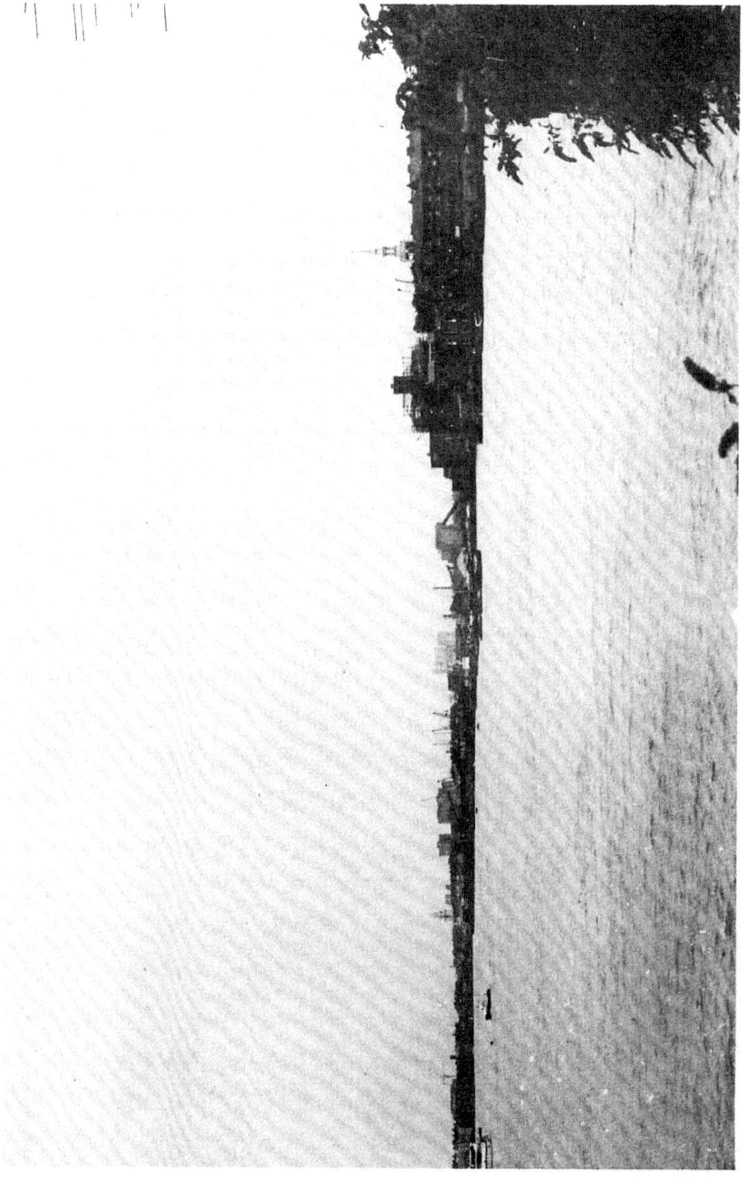

One such know-all wit was called 'The Philadelphia Lawyer' because of knowing everything, then there was the bloke who became known as 'Noddy' because of the woolen hat he wore with a bobble on it just like the famous puppet.

Most people thought it was money for old rope being a docker, and that great amount of money was being 'earned' by them. Well, let me tell you that for the majority of the men this was not so. The old saying being 'It aint what you know it's who you know'.

When I was a docker the 'Bomping on money' as it was called, was 13/– per day. 'Bomping' money was paid to you if you hadn't got a job for the day and you had to go back to the 'Pool' where you handed in your book and got it stamped (Bomped) hence the saying Bomping on. I was allocated to No. 1 Sector which stretched from Scotts Wharf at Shad Thames to Burt Boultons at Belvedere.

We had our 'funny' moments in the docks. Like the time when about twelve of us had got our 'bompers' and we said to Charlie (Bootsy) "Are we all invited round for a cup of tea". Of course Charlie, not taking us serious, said yes. So all of us went to his home, (having got cars and Charlie only having a push bike), we got there before he did. His wife came to the door in answer to our knock and we all said that Charlie had invited us round for tea. Was she furious? Just then poor old Charlie comes round the corner on his bike, puffing away, on his 'old Dr. Salter'. Charlie called us a few choice names I can tell you. "But Charlie," we all said "you did invite us". When we left, and knowing Charlie's missus I bet he got a right tongue-lashing.

I was 'tallying' on a ship in the Finland Yard one day, when a stevedore was killed. He had been working on a paper pulp sailing barge and had looked over the side to see if the set was coming over when it struck him on the head and killed him. The Docks is a dangerous industry and there have been quite a few fatalities. One would soon know if anything like this had happened. The docks would come to a standstill and the men would go home for the rest of the day out of respect for one of them.

The only other time that work would come to a halt would be on Xmas Eve. As quite a few dockers would congregate in the pubs at dinnertime and have a drink, it would have been risky to say the least to carry on working.

Dockers could always be counted on to invent new sayings about different things, for instance when the 'A' boats were in at the Surrey at Scruttons the saying was 'Scruttons for buttons' and right they were, I know for I was one of the mugs what was sent there. All they seemed to carry was flour bags, tons of it. Hard work for shirt-buttons plus a very stiff back. All we could get for a days pay for 600 tons of flour with 30 tons of general cargo, even with a seven o'clock would be £6.18s. One time the whole gang blew the job and they all got 3 days suspension. Luck would have it that it just so happened it was Derby Day and they all went to the races. When you were sent shipside, you were on continuity until your hold was finished and then you would get your book back so that you could shape somewhere else.

The 'pen' in the Surrey was a rather large sombre place. Stone floors, like a prison without bars and the saying among the dockers 'abandon hope all ye who enter here'. A favourite trick of the 'pool' was to keep you waiting till about 8.15 then throw all the windows open and say over the loudspeakers, "All books in". At the same time in would come the coaches which would take you to other sectors where the work was. The men hated this as they knew they would be sent to the Albert Docks and could be continuity 2 weeks and maybe more. The ships over there were massive compared to those in the Surrey.

I soon learnt all the tricks from my brother who had a 'C' stamped on his book for clerking. He told me to get one on my book, which I did. At times this came in very handy as the time when we were continuity on Furness Withy and our own job at Brandrams was in the next day, so we went to the office and said we were 'C' men and they gave us our books back. On Saturdays a lot of men used to have what was known as 'tear-outs'. This meant that they would tear out the leaf in their book for that day and hand them into the pen.

    The places where we shaped for work was outside the pool in Redriff Road. There was the P.L.A. Call, Scruttons, Furness Withy, Burt Boultons, Wallaces and other small companies. The PLA Call was outside the Brunswick Yard and the numbers wanted were put up outside the PLA offices. Many a time when I wanted an afternoons work the Bridge would go up at 12.45 and perhaps they wanted 7 men there and there were only 5 men around and you thought you stood a good chance of an afternoons work, and crossing your fingers that the Bridge would hold up any others coming, taking into account that the Greenjackets would have preference on the PLA call, and you had to wait till they were called off and if they needed more you would get taken on.

    When I was shipside at 1 and 3 shed in the Swedish Yard where we was unloading a Navvy Boat (G.S. & N) when for some reason the men decided to work to rule. The Stevedores were working normally, one man out of the gang was going in and out with a barrow, the Top man was having a baby over this and shouted up "whats up" "we have no barrows" we replied. He looked over to where there was about 20 barrows andsaid "what about those", "Sorry" we said "they have no rubber grips and we cannot use them". To add to the confusion the stacker came round from the Brunswick Yard and was told to go back and get another one as one of the stop lights was not working. The cranedriver was not worrying as he was up in the crane reading a paperback.

    Once, on the Jala boat, some Stevedores played a trick on one

THE BRIDGE IN REDRIFF ROAD WHERE DOCKERS AND STEVEDORES WERE CALLED ON

PLA CALL IN REDRIFF ROAD

of their fellow mates who was looking all over for his bike. They had only hooked up to the crane and it was dangling in the air 60ft up. Trouble was, they could not get it down as the crane driver had gone home to dinner.

When there was a dispute along the wharf, you called in what was generally known as 'the air raid committee' the true name being area committee.

One thing I found amusing when working in the docks, was the pigeons that would gather on the shed roof. Saying has it that they were old dockers who had passed on and were watching to see things go right. The place I liked to work was the old Greenland Dock by the Swedish Yard which used to be the old whaling dock. Part of this used to be the Great Howland Dock owned by Mrs. Howland related to the Duke of Bedford. Mrs. Howland had this dock surrounded by trees. How wise this was as there was a terrible storm which sank a lot of ships in the Thames but only 2 ships in the Great Howland were only slightly damaged. The interesting thing was the old whales head they found whilst building the dock which they placed in a cavity in the wall and plated with glass for all to see.

To my mind I cannot recall any man caught smoking on the key or in the sheds as when a policeman was about the cry along the sheds was 'Beadle' and so it was passed all along the dockside 'beadle, beadle' until you could hear the echo and anyone caught smoking after this was either deaf or daffy.

Although I liked working in the Surreys I would rather work along the wharves because the rates of pay was so much higher. One place we always used to finish up was Diniwicks on fish meal or bone meal. I always used to finish up on the pile, me Johnny Lacey, young Reggie Brown, as the paper bags came up the escalator we got them on our shoulders bread and buttering them this way and that way to bind them. Burst ones going down your neck. Still, money not bad! When we used to go to the coffee shop we used to get some funny looks because the smell was terrible!!! On one occasion, with hand on my heart this is true, Charlie Byford said he was not feeling too good and without his knowing someone slipped a Bob Martins in his tea. After he had drunk his tea he said he was feeling a lot better. Charlie was not a bad bloke but he would wear this old overcoat which he used to wear when working at the Archers Flour Wharf and it used to get smothered in flour and when it rained they said it got so stiff that he could stand it up in a corner when he went to bed. Some would call him Bootsy because he also wore large army boots and some would say he was thick as a dockers sandwich.

At Chambers Wharf there was a geezer who was a ringer for old Fred Flintstone.

At Chambers the key foreman was a former docker. Saying has it that if you make a game warden out of a poacher then your troubles are over. How true this saying was as he knew all the tricks that the dockers could get up to and would watch out for them.

My father was an old 'brass tally' man and many were the times that he was lucky if he got a days work. Once he told me that he had the shirt ripped off his back in the rush to get a days work. He and many other dockers used to do the donkey work of the Stevedores in the Surrey Docks clearing the decks on the timber ships by hand lowering the timber over the sides dropping it into the barges. Once the winches were clear they were paid off and the Stevedores took over. The Stevedores were the top dogs before the war, and called the tune. Jobs were picked in the 'Jolly Caulkers' pub opposite the stave yard also the payments for the job, even when I became a docker over 30 years later, I like him, was a casual worker looking for work just like him the only difference I signed on at the pool and received 13s a day whilst he

JOLLY CAULKERS PUB — SURREY DOCKS
WHERE STEVEDORES WOULD GATHER FOR WORK

CAPSTAN AT THE ENTRANCE TO OLD SURREY DOCKS
— LEADING TO LAVENDER YARD

had to sign on as unemployed. Now the dockers are the top dogs in the docks.

Before the steam ships were in operation men used to hang around the docksides hoping to get a days casual work. It was very uncertain as sailing ships, having to rely on the winds to get them where they wanted to go very often did not arrive at the time it was supposed to dock in the port. Sometimes the casual dock worker would be days without any work at all and then when the ships arrived they would work the ships throughout the day and at night as well so that the ships could load up and sail again on the tide.

The old Sailing Clippers would moor alongside the tea warehouses by the Tower of London and with their derricks swinging to and fro bringing sett after sett onto the quay, where dock labourers were waiting with their barrows to take them onto the warehouse to be weighed and sorted to 'mark' by other men.

In the warehouse men were engaged to blend the tea. This was done by hand. First chests of tea from Canton were tipped onto a clean floor then an equal amount of Indian tea. This was mixed with large wooden spaddles and when it was well blended the tea was repacked in the chests ready to be taken by horse and cart to the various shops. Tea was a luxury that only the rich or middle classes could afford and tea caddies with ornate designs of inlaid satinwood or ivory and nacre. It was always a race with the tea Clippers. First home got the best price for their tea this led to lots of competition between the captains of the Clippers and it was no wonder that safety at sea came second in the race against time and the elements of the sea. Most famous of the Clippers was the Taipin and the Cutty Sark.

The Thermopylae and the Cutty Sark were having a race the Cutty Sark having quite a good lead over the Thermopylae when the Cutty Sark lost her rudder and lost the race. The Cutty Sark, the more acknowledged

CUTTY SARK

Monday, 23rd November, 1869, saw the launching of a small clipper ship from the Scott and Linton's shipyard, Dumbarton on the Clyde. Grossing 963 tons, she was to bear the name which would be famous throughout the world — it was the 'Cutty Sark'.

She was not considered to be a big ship even by the standards of the time though her sail plan was lofty. In comparison with the Queen Elizabeth, her mainmast would barely reach the top of the liner's foremost funnel.

The Cutty Sark was only 212 feet in length and 36 feet across the beam with a depth of 21 feet. According to Basil Lubbock, an acknowledged authority of the sail era, the Cutty Sark and its greatest rival, the Thermopylae, were the fastest ships that ever moved through water under sail.

The sail plan of the Cutty Sark was designed by the master draughtsman in her builders yard to give a plain sail area of around 32,000 square feet; when driving her at maximum speed of just over 17 knots, the power developed was equivalent to an engine of 3,000 h.p.

Although she was very fast in the water, the Cutty Sark did not win any race as a tea clipper.

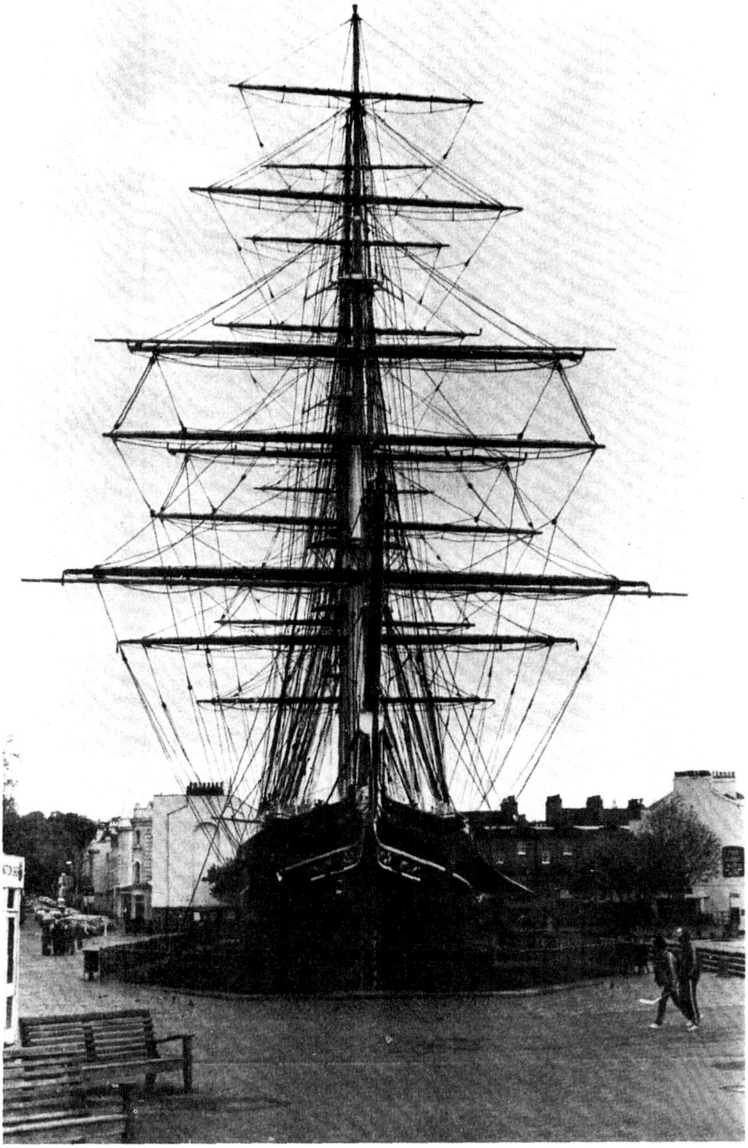

of the Clippers, never did win a race as just after this event the Suez Canal opened up the sea lanes to make the run to the Far East shorter not having to round the Cape of Good Hope, the southernmost tip of South Africa. But the Cutty Sark ended her days on the wool run to Australia.

The Cutty Sark is now in dry dock and can be seen as a museum piece at Greenwich.

The docker had a character that would never be questioned, such was his standing on the dockside. A docker was indeed a proud man and if anyone was injured or a fatality occurred, then the dockers would rally round and a collection would ensue and given to the unfortunate dependants to help augment the meagre offerings from the Board of Guardians.

The Board of Guardians was a group of people (similar to our National Assistance today) who would go to the needy and take particulars of their income and outgoings and assess how much they would allow the family to exist — which would turn out to be a few shillings. This department was called several names by the locals — 'The Parish', 'The R.O.' (short for relieving office) or as some believed it to be the 'Workhouse'. There were no facilities for compensation following a fatal accident in the docks and as the life insurance was only a few pennies per week it was barely enough to bury the deceased.

As in most areas there were villains in the docks — these men would think nothing about stealing cargo where they could. When working on a ship the 'villain' would pass on information to an accomplice who at the dead of night would come alongside the ships in a rowing boat and load up with as much 'cargo' as was safe to carry. These men were known as the 'light horsemen'. So much pilfering was going on that it was in 1792 that the River Police were formed to stop this growing crime. Nevertheless, such were the times that men were ready to risk their necks in order to implement their meagre living standards by this petty pilfering.

Such was the amount that was being stolen that the Government of the day persuaded the shipowners to build enclosed docks to make it that much more difficult for the thieves and on the 3rd of February 1800 a start was made to build the first enclosed dock which was eventually finished and opened on the 27th August, 1802. The first of the Dock police was on duty at the dock gates and the first ship to enter the new dock was the West Indiaman — Henry Addington — complete with the flags of all the European nations — cheers from all the Irish navvies lining the quayside.

At the beginning of the century, a dock worker was lucky if he earned 24/- a week. There were no canteens in the dock yards and men would make their own tea and bring sandwiches made by their wives or mothers. Lucky ones would have beef steak puddings which became known as 'babies heads'. Some men would go to a coffee shop outside of the dock gates and have a pork pie and a pint mug of tea or coffee.

Fruit boats would come in and have to be unloaded at night ready for the Covent Garden Market the next morning and the dockers would work by strong arc lights while the delivery gangs would be standing by to load the horses and carts.

Casual labourers working along the wharves were given an oval brass disc or as it was known 'brass tally' which if they were lucky to get a days work would hand them in to be returned to them when they got their days pay. These 'tallys' were given by the Union to their members. Any man not able to get a days work would have to report to the local Labour Exchange to sign on for a days 'labour money'.

Times were hard for the casuals in the docks and it was only when the war broke out in 1939 that the true value of the dock worker was realised by keeping the flow of unloading ships with vital supplies of food and war requisites.

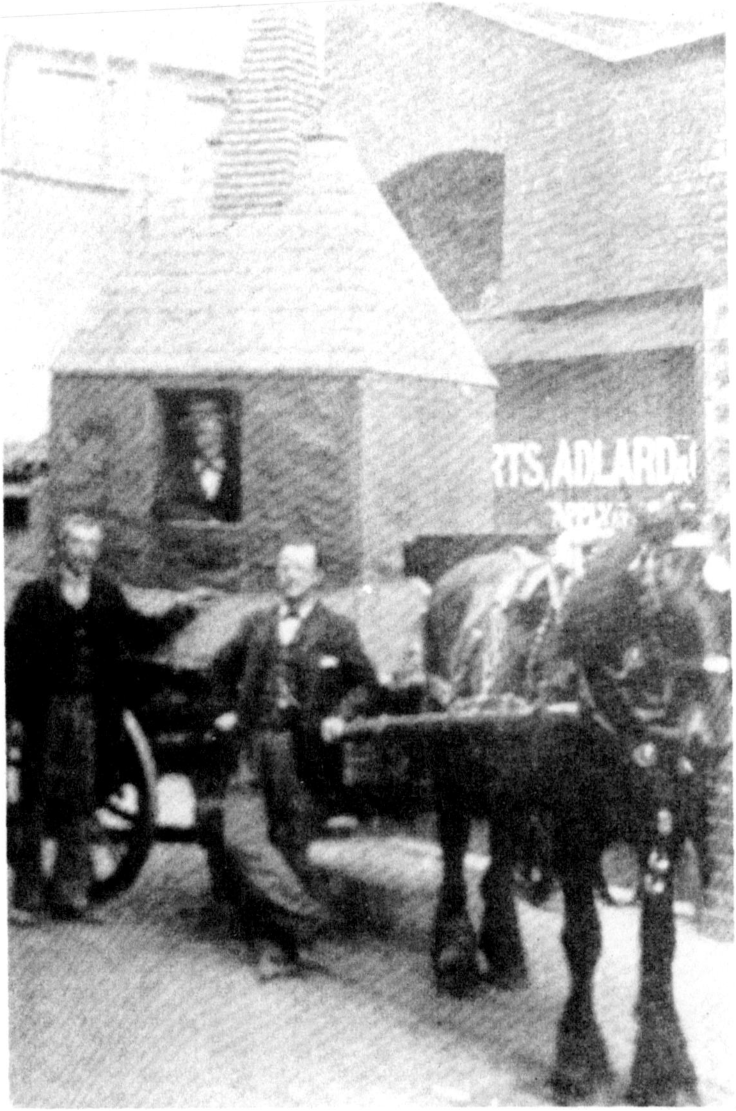
RTS, ADLARD

Car – Watermen and Lightermen Surrey Commercial [illegible]
Trotting Pony – Mr Henry [illegible]

The docks were a prime target for the enemy bombers and the Surrey Docks received one of the worst nights of attention from these bombers when the whole of dockland got the treatment from the Germans wave after wave of them and naturally when it came to the timber yards they went up in smoke in next to no time lighting the whole of London up like it was daylight. It made the Fire of London of 1666 look like a boys scout jamboree party. The heat that radiated from the fires was so hot that it melted the tarmac on the roads some distance away from the actual fire itself. After the incendiaries had done their work in lighting the way for the heavy bombers it did not work out as planned as the bombs which were dropped actually put out some of the fires with there blast of high explosive.

It was not until after the war was over that the dockers gained some respectability when Ernest Bevin registered the dock worker. Men no longer had to sign on at the Labour Exchange when they did not have a days work but were given a fixed amount each day that they did not work and it was then devised that the 'Pool' where the dockers gathered to collect there 'bomping on money'.

It was not until 1967 that Lord Denning was asked to look into the plight of the dockers and devise a way to decasualise the docks so that they had a more permanent living and to get some regular work for the men.

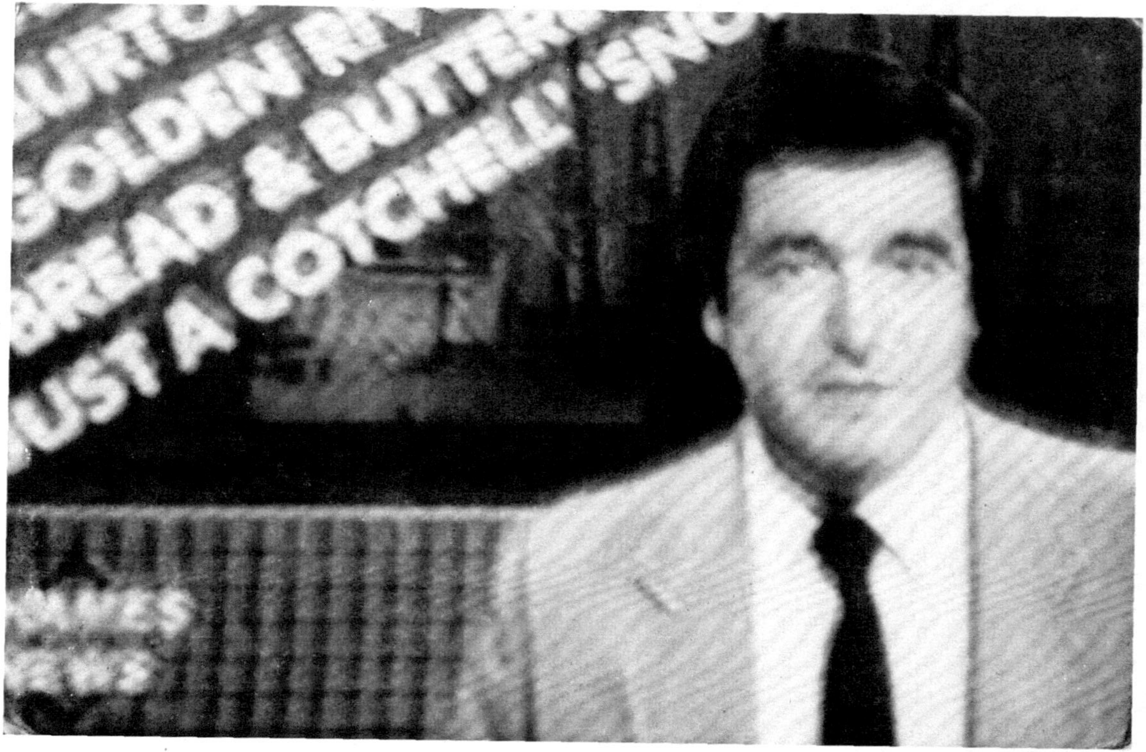
GOLDEN
BREAD & BUTTER
A COTCHELL

CHAPTER 3

SEARCHING FOR THE GOLDEN RIVET

Dockers term for the bottom of the ships hold. When you reached the bottom of the ship the cry would be "I've found the golden rivet".

DUMMY

This was a large heavy raft that was used to hold the ship off the quay — being placed between the ship so that the barges could be placed all round and could be worked on better.

USING THE STICKS

Name given to the winches. The Stevedores preferred to work on the 'sticks' as they maintained they could work faster.

PRO RATA MEN

Men that were hired in addition to the actual men required to do the sorting out of the marks.

DOUBLE BANKING

When a ship was behind time another gang was hired to work in the same hold thus speeding up the work.

HAVING A TEAR OUT

When dockers did not want to be sent out to work on a Saturday they would tear out the end of the week's slip from their book and then hand it in at the pool.

THE PEN

This was the place where the dockers would gather if they had not got any work that day. They would wait until the windows opened and get the call to 'Hand all books in'. If there was any work to be had in other Sectors, then they were sent there by the 'Pool'.

ON THE PENCIL

This was a term used for any docker who was sent out tallying.

RUNNING IN YOUR CARD

On board the ships there were the Ships Clerks and the Merchants Clerks. If a docker was sent out tallying he would make up his card from these clerks — hence running in.

A GANGER

This was a man who was chosen by the Shipworker to pick his men — so many for the Ships holds and so many for the shore work.

TOP MAN

Each hold had a 'Top man' to control the direction for the cranedriver. Standing at the top of the ship in full view of the cranedriver he would signal with his hands — to lower the crane he would hold his right hand palm downward and with an up and down movement — holding his palm upwards for the crane to halt. With clenched fist this would signify to stop or take in the slack line. If he wanted the jib to be raised he would touch the top of his head. To show where he wanted the load to be placed he would point down the hold. When the hooks were attached to the scaleboard he would motion to the cranedriver with arm outstretched palm upwards slowly at first then when it was safe to lift he would quicken the movement of his hand.

STARBOARD

This was the right side of the ship facing forward. The old term was starboard to the right larboard to the left but this caused some confusion and the left was then changed to Port side.

LOWER POOL

Name given to the part of the Thames near Tower Bridge.

O.S.T.

Name taken by tally clerks on all ships. These were the Clerks that worked for the shipping companies and the Merchants and also the Ships Clerks.

COME BACK WHEN THE INK IS DRY ON YOUR BOOK

This was a saying by dockers to young dockers who had not been in the docks for very long and tried to tell older dockers what to do.

THE 'A' BOATS

These were boats that belonged to Scruttons in the Surrey Docks. All the names of the ships began with the letter 'A'.

CARRYING A MAN

Often you would get a man who liked to have a drink or go to the betting office or for some domestic reason disappeared for the afternoon. Rather than give your fellow worker away you would carry on as if he were there.

GOING TO WORK ON A SLIP

When a man was continuity on another job and his usual job

came up for which he normally shaped he would ask a friend for a slip out of his book so that he could go and give his friend the slip out of his book — thus doing a change over and 'going to work on a slip'.

BEING RUN

A term for breaking continuity when he would be penalised by the Pool — being suspended for so many days and perhaps being fined by the Union.

EYES UP

This term was used by the 'Top Man' to men working in the Holds of the ship to make them move out of the way when a load was dangerous or falling out.

MUGGO

When this was heard from the Top Man it would denote the time for a tea-break.

CUSTOM AND PRACTICE

Term used for any thing that although not the correct thing but because it was usually done it followed that it was acceptable.

SHORT SEA TRADERS

Term used for wharves and suchlike.

DEEP SEA TRADERS

This was the term for the big ships that go into the docks.

NAVVY BOATS   General Steam Navigation Boats.

LEFT ROASTING
Term used to denote that you were the only person on a call that had not been taken on for work.

REHOUSING
Men taken on to shift cargo in the sheds to make room for fresh cargo from the ships.

DOUBLE BOMPER
Men who had got their first 'bomper' were allowed to wait till 9 o'clock to get a second one to save them coming back at 1 o'clock.

JOB AND FINISH
When a ship did not have much cargo the dockers would work the holds until the job was done, and getting a double stamp on their books.

OVERNIGHT SELECTIONS
Men who were friends or drinking partners of the Gangers who were assured of a job on the call.

GREENACRES
Name given to any type of accident that occurred in the docks i.e. things falling out of setts whilst being lifted out of the ships hold.

BOMPING ON
Men who were not successful in getting a days work and had to go to the pool to get their books stamped for that day.

BEADLE
Dock police.

OVERSIDE
Loading into the barges from the ship. The Port side being the inside and the Starboard the outside.

THE BIG HOUR
This was the name that dockers gave to an hours overtime mainly the five to six hours overtime (5 o'clock to 6 o'clock).

A SHORT NIGHT
Working on the ship from 5 o'clock to 10 o'clock allowing the men to be able to turn out for a days work the next day.

ALL NIGHTER
Men who worked the ship all night until it finished. These men would be given the next day off and paid for it.

TURN OUT MONEY
This was extra money given for men who worked outside of their normal Sector.

SHAPING FOR WORK
This was a term used for men who knew where a job was and went onto the call.

THE PLA (A) MEN
These men were always on the PLA call and were eventually placed in 'A' positions and were given priority on the call.

DAY WORK

Men who were paid at 'day time rate'. This work was mainly done by the older men such as sweeping sheds and quays the only sweetener was that they were paid till 7 o'clock to help make their money up.

THE PITCH

The place on the quay where the dockers worked.

SCALE BOARDS

Name given to the large heavy boards with steel eyelets on each corner for the crane hooks to be inserted when the boards were loaded up for stowing into the holds.

A DDH

This was an abbreviation for a double dinner hour which was when a docker would work through his dinner hour to get a ship finished early. It meant that the docker would be finished early as well.

UP THE ROAD

Docker saying when the job was finished.

DRAGGING OUT

On the big ships the run in between the hatches went under so far that double steel bonds were attached to the hooks of the crane and the cargo had to be dragged out from under. This could be quite dangerous at times.

COLD POT   Name given to the cold storage depots.

SNOW BANGING

When working in the 'cold pot' men would be employed to bang the ice from the refrigeration pipes. This would be double day work for the men.

BLOWING A JOB

When a man wanted to break continuity by not turning up at the job he was on especially when this could mean that he could shape for a job he was a regular on. This would be followed up with a certificate to say he wasn't well that day or that he had overdone it i.e. was late. When this occured a man was sent from the pool to cover the job.

RUNNING A MAN

One union member taking another before the Committee for infringeing the Rules.

AIR RAID COMMITTEE

A popular term for the Area Committee which would be sent when a dispute on a ship occured.

DIRTY MONEY

Extra money that dockers received when handling dirty cargo.

WORKING ON THE BUOYS

When a ship was moored in midstream and you were taken on board by boats from the shore.

A SHOW OF CARDS

Any Union member could call for a 'show of cards' a 'White

Ticket holder" (TGWU) had preference over a holder of a 'Blue Ticket' (Stevedores Union).

STROOM BOATS

These were small Dutch coasters that were often in and out of the small wharves and unloading general cargo and reloading again before sailing. Many of these ships were family owned.

LOCK UPS

These were compounds kept aside for goods and personal effects to be passed by the Customs Officers.

SUFFERENCE AND FREE TRADE WHARVES

These were set up many years ago to help out the 'Legal Quays' as they were known such as Billingsgate etc. who found that they could not cope with the amount of shipping at the time.

COCK CHAFFERS

Years ago when the cranes in some docks had to be worked by men who would walk inside a big wheel on the quays. This would be geared to a jib and by walking round and round this would work the crane.

WORKING TO RULE

When there was a dispute on a ship or on the docks dockers would not go for an all out strike but would work to rule which meant that they would only do what was the Unions recommended i.e. no overtime or job and finish etc. Small things that could disrupt the work i.e. if a barrow did not have rubber grips the work would cease until a regulation barrow was found or if an electric stacker did not have its regulation lights on it then until it was repaired it could not be used thereby causing slower work.

THE GOLDEN MILE

This was a term for the stretch of Redriff Road where the PLA worked on plywood and would earn very good money.

LIBERTY BOATS

These were the boats that were bought by the Greeks from the Americans after the last war. These ships were constructed in two halves for speed.

THICK AS A DOCKERS SANDWICH

This saying goes back to the days when the docker would take his own dinner to work usually very thick slices of bread, margerine and cheese which they would have with their pint of ale at dinner time.

ANOTHER DAY ANOTHER DOLLAR

This was a saying that a docker had when it had been a bad day and they looked forward to earning another 'dollar' the next day. This was usually followed by saying that 'you can't make a good day out of a bad one'.

LIGHTS

This was a term used for calling over the side of the ship to attract the attention of the lighterman.

BLUES   Name for a Stevedore who held a blue Union card.

WHITES
> Name for a docker who was a white Union card holder.

PIGEONS
> These birds that were forever on the shed roof — These were supposedly old dockers who had passed on but were keeping an eye out over the docks.

SECTORS
> Dockers were allocated to numbered sectors — 1 to 7. A docker could only shape for work in the sector number shown on his card.

LEGS
> These were chains which were attached to a large ring that had hooks on the other end, when hanging on the crane it looked like a pair of legs.

SHOREWAYS
> Anything going from ship to shore.

PIPER
> This was a term used by dockers for a man who was not rated or a man who was not pulling his weight.

SWINGING THE LEAD
> Although this was an old Naval term it was 'borrowed' and used as another term for a piper.

IN THE SADDLE   Often used to indicate whose turn it was to buy the teas.

GUNTERS PERMS OR JEEPS

These were the men that came into the docks after decasualisation took place — the Minister was Ray Gunter.

ON A PROMISE

If a job was not paying well you were given a promise of a 7 o'clock to make up the money.

STOPPING THE SHIP

When a dispute occured on board a ship and the 'air raid committee' were called in while waiting for them all work was suspended.

DOUBLE DAY WORK

When a job was poorly paid a promise of double time pay to the men to get them working on the cargo and unload the ship.

TALL IN THE SADDLE

Name given to a man who was very tall.

SNORTER

A single rope used mostly on paper reels this was capable of holding 15 cwt. Up to 15 cwt. could be used at one time when unloading bacon.

DOUBLE STROP

A continuous rope capable of taking a strain of 30 cwt.

RUB DOWN
When being stopped at the dock gates by the Dock Police they would rub you down to see if you had any stolen goods.

DEAL PORTERS
These were men who worked exclusively on the timber boats. If they were not employed because there were no timber boats in they could work on a dockers call.

TOE RAGGERS
Name applied to the Corn Porters. When working down the ships hold they would tie sacking round their boots to stop the corn from getting into them.

THE GOLD COAST
Nickname for the New Fresh Wharf just below London Bridge on the north side. Men would earn fantastic wages when working on the tomato boats.

OVER THE WATER
When being sent to other sectors.

TURNIP BASHER
Term applied to the dockers at Tilbury.

THE SURREY
Popular name for the Surrey Commercial Docks.

HITTING THE CEILING
Same as the call of 'Iv'e found the ceiling'. When the men had

reached the bottom of the ship.

THE JOLLY CAULKERS

An old public house where Stevedores would meet to be allocated work and receive pay when finished.

RUN OF THE MILL

Something quite ordinary.

IT AINT WOT YER KNOW BUT WHO YER KNOW

This is an old dockers saying for drinking pals of the gangers who tend to give work to their drinking pals, thus they had an advantage on those who maybe didn't drink or socialise with the gangers.

DOLLY MIXTURE

Sets that were made up of various items.

DONKEY MAN

Man on the ship working the winches.

THE ROYALS

Name given to men who worked in the Royal Albert Docks.

OVER THE WEST

Name given to the West India Docks.

COFFIN BOATS

Ships that brought the special boards used for coffin making.

LONER

A man who kept himself to himself

PULLING A STROKE

This alluded to any docker who by certain actions by him 'did the dirty' on his mates.

TUPPENY FUND

This fund was made up from the few pence that could not be divided between the men when making up the bill for a job. This was put into a 'kitty' and reserved for dockers who are in distressed circumstances. This particular fund now runs into millions.

FOR AND AFT

Front and rear of ships.

TOGGLED

When a set gets caught under the gunnel of the ship or is obstructed in any other way.

BURTON

When dockers are loading down into the ships hold in pairs if one of them wanted to place an item in a direction that was opposite to the way they were working he would say to his partner 'put this one on the burton'.

BREAD AND BUTTERED

This means binding the stack i.e. first one direction then the next layer in another.

LYKES BOATS
Ships belonging to the famous American family after which all the ships were named.

HATCHES
These were normally lifted off by the crew of the ships unless they were too heavy then they were lifted by the crane driver.

ON WHEELS
This was applied to any dockers who came to work either by bycycle or car.

TOM PEPPER
Dockers name for a person who could lie his way out of an awkward situation.

MUSHROOMS
Name applied to some of the bollards that held the mooring ropes of the ships.

SHIPS PILOT
These men were from Trinity House and trained to bring the ships up river as a ship could not progress up river without one to guide him along the river.

SIX HEADER
When piling bagwork you would put four longways and two across reversing the positions on each layer thus binding the stack.

FIVE BAR GATE

When doing a checking job, to keep a correct count you would use the five bar gate system. This meant that each count you would mark an upright stroke and when you had four you would on the next count put a stroke across on an angle thus making a gate. This made it easier to make a final count at the end.

DANGER MONEY

Extra money paid to the men when working on hazardous cargo.

MONEY FOR OLD ROPE

Easy jobs that pay well.

THE MAMMOTH

A giant floating crane for lifting several hundred tons at a time into the ships from the quay.

BLACKED

This denotes that the cargo is in dispute i.e. blacked or not to be handled until further notice.

BLUE PETER

Flag denoting that the ship is ready to sail.

STRIKING THE FLAG

When ships entered the ports they always showed the flag of the country they were entering.

SALVAGE WORK

Work carried out by the dockers on holds that had been

either flooded out by water or had a fire on board thus damaging the cargo.

LASKIS, DAGOS, JOHNSONS, MATELOTS AND FROGGIES
Names applied to the seamen on the ships.

FRIENDLY LEAD
When a man was accidently killed there would be a whip round in the local pub for the man's dependants.

MAN ON THE BEACH
Term applied to a Quay Foreman.

DOWN HOLERS
Men working on the ships down the holds.

LOOP HOLES
Men working from the wharves inside the warehouse, usually unloading barges.

SAILING BARGES
These were barges which were powered by sail. These were usually red. They carried paper pulp or timber.

GENERAL CARGO
Term for a ship carrying a mixed cargo.

DAY AND OUT
This applied to a ship that had very little to unload and maybe meant only half an hours work. A docker would then do the job

and be 'up the road'.

FLAG BOATS

These appertained to the Paper reel boats that came in at Convoys Wharf Deptford.

MISSING THE TIDE

Term applied to a ship that cannot come into dock as the tide was away and therefore the water too shallow.

PIER HEAD

Part of the dock which juts out by the lock gates.

IN THE LOCK

When waiting for a ship to berth it was often said that she's in the lock meaning the ship was caught in between the lock gates.

WE'RE WINNING

An expression that was used to denote that a job was nearly finished.

CATCHING A BRIDGER

Often an excuse used when getting back to work late or for not turning up when on continuity. There were the swing bridges between several docks and when waiting for ships or barges to pass through these bridges the roads would be closed up. This would be more than nuisance value if you were trying to get to a call that would bring a fair days pay.

D8 OR D20

This was a form that was sent to a docker who had committed some infringement of Rule and had been suspended. These were sent by recorded delivery so that the excuse of not receiving the letter no longer applied.

OLD DOCKERS SAYING

The rain comes in with the tide and goes out with it.

BRASS TALLY MEN

Years ago before the last World War dockers were given a brass tally, oval in shape which they would hand in when given a job and have it returned when collecting their pay. If they did not get a days work they would have to sign on at their local Labour Exchange.

THE DOCKERS TANNER

This was the sixpence (tanner) a day that Ben Tillitt fought for years to get for the dockers. At this time many people were sympathetic towards the dockers.

CEILING OF A SHIP

Strange as it may seem but the bottom of a ship was called the ceiling and when unloading if you heard the cry "I can see the ceiling" then you knew that the hold was nearly finished.

MAKING A BREAK

Once the dockers got down the dold of a ship they would dig down into the cargo to make room for the first scaleboard to get in thereby making it easier to work the load.

COVER UP
When it rained the Top Man would shout to the gangs working below and they would then come out of the hold and put the hatches on similarly when it stopped raining the call would be to "uncover".

THE QUEENS HOLIDAY
Dockers were always given a Saturday off in honour of the Queens Birthday.

THE MAIN HOLD
This was always amidships and the best gang always got this hold.

THE FRENCHMAN
Name given to a very large French boat laden with rubber bales which Stevedores loaded into large nets. Many times as the net came over the ship, one would escape from the net and as they weighed around 2 cwt. when they hit the deck or quay there was pandemonium as you could not tell which way the bale was going to bounce. Until it stopped there was utter panic.

THE JALA BOAT
These were large Indian boats which came onto the Furness Withy berths loaded mainly with tea but carrying some other general cargo.

SKIMMING
Term used where marks on cargo had to be sorted out and if you could not get the right marks wanted first then you would 'skim' across the hold sorting marks to make a break.

THE DRINK
　　Term for the water in the docks similarly the 'beach' would denote the dock or quay.

PLUGS
　　Refridgerated ships did not have hatches but insulated plugs to keep the cold in. These were lifted by cranes as they were very heavy.

REGISTRATION BOOK
　　This was a book that contained 52 slips (pages). Each slip had to be rubber stamped (bomped) by an Employer.

PAY BOOK
　　This book contained numbered slips which the docker handed to the Employer. The slip would be torn out when collecting the pay for the week that the number on the slip denoted.

JOCKEY
　　Name given to a stacker driver.

BEACH COMBER
　　Day worker employed to keep the quays clear of broken pallets and debris.

BOGEY
　　A four wheeled barrow for landing sets from the ship to take into the sheds.

JACK Long blades on wheels that could be raised up under the pallets for removal.

LONG ARM
This applied to any object that was long and narrow and instead of holding it between, you would hold it either side and put it into place.

PULLING A FLANKER
Dockers who would break continuity and not get a D20.

ON THE STONES
Another word for being on the call.

JETTY
Part of the quay that juts out when the tide is away.

GEAR MAN
Man employed to distribute any working equipment i.e. strops, legs, bonds etc.

SHANKS PONY
Dockers description to denote that he had walked all the way to work.

WORKING FOR LOVE
Dockers saying for a job that pays poor money.

PAD HOOKS
Hand hooks — one held in each hand oval shaped with spikes so as not to tear the sacks which held either flour, corn etc.

SHIPSIDE
　　Being on continuity to a ships hold.

ON THE BLOCK
　　A simple job. Docker walking alongside a stacker driver with a wooden block, a length of string to put in between plywood so that the stacker could get his blades in to lift.

TWEEN DECKS
　　In between the decks of the hold.

CRACK AN EGG
　　Term a Top Man would use to the crane driver when he wanted the set to be lowered gently.

A PLUMPER
　　Another name for a hundredweight (cwt.).

HOBSON JOBSON DAY
　　Old saying meaning a gathering or marches by dockers.

A 'C' MAN
　　A docker who was considered unfit to carry out heavy work and would usually be given light duties. His book would have a 'C' stamped on it.

JUMBO
　　This was a term used for working two winches together to lift very heavy cargo.

JUST A COTCHELL
A small amount of cargo.

DOCKERS SLANG
Dockers slang is not much different to the Cockney slang except that most of the slang dockers appertained to the actual work. Where it did not, then the slang could be used in everyday talk outside of the docks to be entwined with the cockney language. This is not so unusual as most dockers were cockneys and had a lot to do with the origins of the slang.

PONY RIDING OR SUCKING THE MONKEY
In the old days dockers working in the Bonded warehouses would make a funnel of stiff paper and putting this in the bungholes would then suck up the drink.

BABIES HEADS
This refers to beef steak and kidney puddings made by the dockers wives and made in round pudding basins. When tipped out these looked like a baby's head.

ON THE MACE OR MAKE
This refers to a man who was fiddling or stealing goods from the docks.

PUSHING THE BOAT OUT
A saying when it was any mans turn to buy the tea.

WET THE BABY'S HEAD
To treat a workmate to a drink.

TO BUTTER UP
To be extra nice to another for a favour.

A DODDLE
An easy job.

HUFFLING
Working a barge by means of an oar.

SWORN WEIGHTER OR SWORN METER
A man who is sworn in before a court of law and also to weigh or measure goods between buyer and seller.

DONKEYWORK
To work as hard as the donkeys that used to work the derricks in the old days.

THAMES BORLEY MEN
Men catching shrimps in the Thames.

BREAD AND BUTTER DAYS
Days when a docker would pick up a job that paid very little — just enough to 'put butter on the bread'.

BEING STRIPED
When another did you a wrong turn when the other dockers found out they would say you're being striped.

DUNNAGE
Timber that was used to stow cargo upon.

EVERLASTING STAIRCASE
This referred to the treadmill that was never-ending, and worked the cranes before motorisation.

TO BE A 'WRONG UN'
Term used for anyone with bad habits.

PAL
Taken from the Gipsy language meaning friend or work mate.

TROUBLE & STRIFE/ THE OTHER HALF
Both these mean a wife.

ALL A BUBBLE
Referring to a person who gets excited easily.

PHILADELPHIA LAWYER
This term was used to indicate another who thinks he knows all the answers — in other words a clever dick.

HOLE IN THE WALL
Term applied to any cutting in the Embankment Wall. Prime example is the one at nearby Tower Bridge called Shad Thames.

COCK A DEAF UN
To totally ignore a person.

COME A CROPPER
To make a mess of something.

ELBOW GREASE
>To apply ones energy to hard work.

TO FLY THE FLAG OF DISTRESS
>When a mans shirt tail could be seen flapping from a hole in his trousers.

TO KICK IN
>To put money into a collection.

TO SLAG A PERSON
>To run a person down.

LIGHT HORSEMEN OR SCUFFLERS
>Thieves who stole from the barges or ships.

SCOTCH MIST
>When something was pointed out and the person took no notice then one would say "whats that a scotch mist".

LOAD OF TOFFEE
>This appertains to anyone talking rubbish.

FREEMANS QUAY
>A wharf in Tooley Street where drivers and porters were given free drinks.

FREEMANS
>Something for nothing.

QUEER THE PITCH
When a person does something to make another persons place/work go wrong.

FALL OUT OF BED
This refers to anyone who thought he was on to a good thing and it turns out to be otherwise.

TO HAVE A POP
This means to argue with another.

SHAYO
Each man on the same bill would receive equal money. Michael O'Shea only had one eye and saw everything the same.

ICE CREAM MAN
This was the official rat-catcher. So nicknamed because he was dressed in white.

BANG WALLEY
The men would agree to share the wage bill equally.

NONNER
Was a non-union man who would hang around in the hope that should there not be enough men on the call he would be taken on.

IDLERS or POKERS
Men who hung around the dock gates hoping for a days' work.

MUD PILOTS
    Tugs that brought ships into the docks.

DUMB BARGES
    Barges towed by tugs.

DOLLY BAGS
    Silk stockings carried by men who worked in the tea warehouses who would fill the stockings with tea and it would hang down inside the legs of their trousers unseen.

TOKE
    Food.

TICKET MEN
    These were men who had a ticket thus ensuring them of regular work and who were also privileged above the casual men.

OLD NELL GOT IT ALL!
    This refers to the days when an employer would give the ganger extra money to be shared among the men thus ensuring a good days work from them. Often the ganger would pocket this extra cash and if queried by his gang would say, "Old Nell got it all" — meaning the proverbial carrot dangled before the donkey!